T0209356

Building Relationships

A Christian Perspective
on Social Coexistence

GEORGE VINCENT AMAGNOH
PhD, MFA, MAIA, BA Hons.

BUILDING RELATIONSHIPS
A CHRISTIAN PERSPECTIVE ON SOCIAL COEXISTENCE

iUniverse books may be ordered through booksellers or by contacting:

iUniverse
1663 Liberty Drive
Bloomington, IN 47403
www.iuniverse.com
844-349-9409

ISBN: 978-1-6632-2519-1 (sc)
ISBN: 978-1-6632-2520-7 (e)

Library of Congress Control Number: 2021916034

Print information available on the last page.

iUniverse rev. date: 08/03/2021

To my inspirer, protector, and healer, the Holy Spirit

To all parents in households and families of
the Christian faith across the world

To leaders of social groups and organizations,
spiritual and secular alike

You are the perfect bridge, linking our
tomorrow to greater social coexistence,
worthy of God's approval.

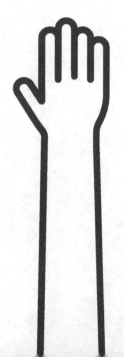

CONTENTS

ILLUSTRATIONS

PREFACE

Personally, I believe God doesn't just invest His power in a person, neither does He heal, grant ideas, or give visions without the ultimately purpose of His investment benefiting His people in return. The Bible says, "But as many as received Him, to them He gave the right to become children of God, to those who believe in His name" (John. 1:12). God's main desire for humankind is to grant us power to perform to the benefit of His church and the glorification of His name. However, the granting of that power is dependent upon our commitment to His will, that is, to receive and believe in His Son. The truth is, God associates and relates only to those who commit and abide by His will. God's Son, Jesus Christ, affirms this truth, saying, "For whoever does the will of God is My brother and My sister and mother" (Mark 3:35). Consequently, we can readily deduce that committing to God's will and being of relevance to His kingdom is paramount to our being recognized as children of the Most High—God.

Another basic truth about God's dealings with us is that He does not start work with humans uninvited. However, when He sees committed hearts, He works with such individuals. Every engagement of God is a divine contract, and like all His contracts, He will see it through to its conclusion, no matter how long it takes in our eyes. The evidence of this truth is enshrined in the pages of this book. How we relate, receive, create, and practice the God-given value of love in our families and with our neighbors must be informed by the understanding that He first loved us by giving His only Son as a sacrifice to atone for our sins. We must see His immense love and apply it to our relationships—how we recreate, practice, interact, and treat one another regardless, would be a testament to the truth about His love.

In my constant search for the truth about what God's love act really means, the Holy Spirit granted me insight into love and what it takes to craft and build relationships. *Love*, not as a word reflecting fondness based on human lust and kindness-returned but love, as a God-inspired acronym—leave, overcome, venture, and empathize. Once operational—understood, practiced, and seen—through the prism of a pointillist ethos, the four words create a social-relational cordiality, devoid of bitterness, regret, and rancor. In these pages lies the full consciousness of how simple God's love is, yet deeper, wider, and more intriguing than you might ever imagine.

Have a happy reading, my brother and my sister, and endeavor to be the link our families, and communities need to experience a true godly love.

ACKNOWLEDGMENTS

I am very much grateful and thankful to my first love, the Almighty God, for granting me insight and direction, by way of the Holy Spirit, during the entire course of putting the contents of this volume together. You are truly an awesome God. To my spiritual father, Rev. Bismark Osei Akomeah, Head Pastor of the Jesus Power Ministry, Columbus, Ohio, and his deputy, Rev. Ofosu Atta, I say thank you so much; your biblical teachings and programs over the years have been so profound—opened up my heart and steered my mind to a better understanding of God's Word and nature—and empowered me to draw closer to the Most High God.

I owe a depth of gratitude and thanks to my second love, Janet, a perfect, and insightful gift from the Lord Almighty, and my beautiful children—the three E's—Edwin, Edwina, and Emmanuela. Your reassurances allowed me to slip out of the house, sometimes Nicodemus-ly, to put my thoughts together on paper. You are collectively my inspiration and the warmth that surrounds me in my coldest moments.

To my cousin, Dr. Cornelius Nuworsoo, I say thank you so much for helping to brainstorm a fitting title for the book. And to a great friend and brother, Jonathan Kekeli, I say thank you. As William Shakespeare would put it, your heart is filled with "the milk of human kindness" (Shakespeare 1605), such that no matter how odd the hour in which I called, you were eager and ready to give a listening ear to my organized thoughts, while making critical contributions along the way. You truly made a memorable mark on this finished product.

To my little sister, Matilda, who passed into glory in December 2019, I thank you posthumously. Your words of encouragement continue to be my life's motivation. I also posthumously thank my parents, Anastasia and George K. N. Amagnoh, for modeling behaviors that echoed in many ways what God wants His children to be like on earth.

Finally, to you my readers around the world, I say thank you, for accepting me into your homes and families. I pray that as you read these pages, the good Lord will grant you wisdom, knowledge, understanding, revelation, and discernment, in addition to a warm heart. I thank God for opening your hearts and minds to a renewed spiritual and social-pathway, capable of creating a social-relational culture that meets the relational challenges of today's world. Together, we can build our relationships, based on the uncompromising love act of God and in peaceful coexistence with one another. Once again, I thank you all.

SECTION 1
Introduction

The contents of this book are discussed in six distinct but interrelated sections. Diagrams that illustrate the pointillist-relational ethos of value creation and practice are taken from my previous publication, *What Do U See When U See Us? ... A Pointillist Perspective* (2014). Section 1 of the book introduces the reader to a need for the book, while sections 2–5 deal with the *what, how, when,* and *who* questions pertaining to the pointillist-relational ethos of value creation and practice within families and society. Section 6 concludes the book with the need to be mindful of the relational value choices we make on behalf of our families, society, and ourselves. The sections are therefore laid out as follows:

Section 1—Introduction
Section 2—Relational Value: *What* (Is It)?
Section 3—Relational Value: *How* (Does It Happen)?
Section 4—Relational Value: *When* (Should It Be Practiced)?
Section 5—Relational Value: *Who* (Uses It)?
Section 6—Conclusion

It was a beautiful morning in the spring of 2008. I was right in the middle of my morning shower when I heard, deep in my spirit, the word *pointillism*. At that moment, I was convinced the Holy Spirit had just spoken to me, reminding me of what I already had in hand, as a teacher of the studio arts. Months prior to that fateful morning, I had been praying and seeking the face of the Lord for divine direction. Yes, I needed God to grant me an idea worthy of making my doctoral research unique, and that morning I received the answer to my prayers. From that moment of divine inspiration, pointillism became the conceptual framework that would inform the proposal and execution of my doctoral dissertation.

Seven years after that divine inspiration, I had yet another prompting from the Holy Spirit. This time, it was in the quiet office environment of the Jesus Power Assembly of God Church in Columbus, Ohio, where I serve and assist in the day-to-day administrative work of the church. The encounter that day was revealing in many ways, as I did not have the least intent to use the "Pointillist-Multicultural Activation Model," or P-MAM (Amagnoh 2014) as a teaching tool within Christendom. All along, it was my aim to use the framework in academia—schools and colleges—to inform and help improve social relationships among students from diverse sociocultural backgrounds. Yet there I was, in the quietude of my thoughts, wondering what exactly God had brought me into a church office environment to do, after having spent over three decades within the corridors of academia. Then, that still voice broke through again, this time with a command: "Use P-MAM to teach my people," the voice said. I turned around swiftly in my chair, expecting to see someone behind me, but there was no one, only a wall. Seconds later, I heard the voice again, with the same command.

Suddenly, I realized that God had given me an assignment—to reorganize P-MAM as an education and instructional tool for His people. As I struggled to come to terms with this command, many questions flooded my mind: *Could this be the reason why He brought me to this church and into this office? Will I be able to use that which was developed purposely for academia in the kingdom of God?*

While contemplating these and many more questions, it occurred to me that God is the controller of our destinies. He alone holds all wisdom and knowledge, and if He has assigned me this project, then He also would guide me to develop the ideas. I told myself that if the God of yesterday, today, and tomorrow has done it before, then He can do it again. All I had to do was ask Him in prayer and supplication. And that is what I did and continued to do.

This book, *Building Relationships: A Christian Perspective on Social Coexistence*, is the result of the divine command received. It discusses the subject of creating and practicing social-relational values in a multicultural world so that our relationships in a world that is socially and culturally diverse can have meaning and give joy to our hearts, regardless of our differences. It places emphasis on the home and the immediate family, where our individual social lives begin, as intended by God. Besides, the book presents a unique insight into how a pointillist viewpoint may be activated in our homes, such that our families may become strong social and spiritual institutions, fashioned through the love of our Creator, God. Therefore, it is my hope that the book will serve as a social-relational guide for parents and families around the world—ministers and leaders of all faith-based organizations, educators in public and private schools of ministry and theological seminaries, lay workers in God's vineyard, such as department heads and heads of ministries and leaders of social groups, organizations, and societies in and outside the church.

Furthermore, the book may also serve as a guide in shaping our families to live fulfilled relationships and as change agents for ourselves and our children. It is to help us become credible examples for the world to see and follow, particularly those desiring to give their lives to God but who are waiting and watching us, as believers, for reassurance. We owe it to God to be loving and living examples so that through us, others may know who He is and what He stands for, through the values we uphold in our homes and with our neighbors, regardless of ethnicity, culture, or race. Finally, this book is my humble response to God's divine instruction, intended to create a tangible way forward, while bridging the social-relational divide through the introduction of a pointillist-relational ethos that resonates with what God intends for His people, whom He loves.

Pointillism is an artistic theory developed by Georges Seurat in the 1700s (Herbert 1991). It became a well-known and popular technique used by studio artists, particularly painters, in the nineteenth and twentieth centuries. Developed from studies into the visible spectrum of light, Seurat used the technique to paint with colored dots of red, blue, and green, placed side by side on canvas, in varying degrees of value and intensity. In my case, guided by divine direction, I researched and recognized how obscure the pointillist concept has remained in educational studies literature and, most importantly, in social and multicultural literature. I decided, then, to search and marry pointillism to an already established educational theory in order to make a compelling case. Finally, I settled on using John Dewey's *instrumentalism* (Amagnoh 2014; Eldridge 1998). The subtle combination of pointillism and instrumentalism led to the creation of an all-new socio-cultural model, dubbed the Pointillist-Multicultural Activation Model, or P-MAM. The model was created with one purpose only: to be my humble contribution to multicultural and cross-cultural literature within the field of educational studies.

The relevance of using P-MAM to guide families in today's diverse and multicultural environment cannot be overstated because it is undeniable that a strong, safe, multicultural society depends greatly on the social-relational strength and character of its individual homes and families. Similarly, the strength of the family relies greatly on the character of its leaders—the parents. Therefore, every parent has an important role to play in building a strong family relationship, grounded in a healthy interpersonal communication with others within the family, as well as the larger community. Parents, together with members of their immediate families, represent the basic building blocks of the community and society. The community—and, for that matter, society—would lose the battle against the forces that seek to divide and destroy when parents and their family (communities' basic building block) gives in to such forces. In this regard, I find it critical to examine and discuss social-relational value as a crucial ingredient in building sound relationships in the home and beyond.

Our God is a faithful God, and the evidence of His faithfulness is revealed through this book. What you are about to read is the result of His work through one of His children. God works with anyone who is ready to commit time in His vineyard with an open heart and mind—anyone who diligently asks Him to perfect his or her social and relational imperfections. Therefore, like wet, soft clay in the hands of a potter, I have given myself up to be used by the master artisan Himself, to reach His people with His message and for the glorification of His name.

THE SIGNIFICANCE OF RELATIONSHIPS
IN THE FAMILY AND SOCIETY

Relationship is of great importance to God and to every family of this world.

It is God's sole desire for all of humankind, His creation, to work out a strong and unique relationship, first with Him and second with themselves—a relationship that is absolute and bonded by the constant act of a personal fellowship with Him, the Godhead. (I'll discuss the act of a personal fellowship in greater detail later.) The apostle John lamented greatly over the absence of our relationship with God, saying, "He was in the world, and the world was made through Him, and the world did not know Him. He came to His own, and His own did not receive Him" (John 1:10–11). Cordiality, consistency, and receptiveness are essential in a relationship. Therefore, I can't even begin to imagine how painful it must have been for God the Father to send His Son, who with open arms came to those He believed to be His own, just to be rejected.

Jesus Christ, who is God the Son, made the issue of building relations very clear in His teachings while on earth, saying, "I am the vine, you are the branches. He who abides in Me, and I in him, bears much fruit; for without Me you can do nothing" (John 15:5). As individuals, our concern for one another becomes greater when we forge strong relationships. The central truth is that building a strong relationship enhances the bonds of trust and belief in one another, which ultimately leads to greater confidence in production, reproduction, and success in life. Therefore, in the true spirit of the word, relationships must transcend families and ethnic and racial allegiances because where true relationship and love exists, family and cultural boundaries melt away.

THE CREATION STORY AND RELATIONAL VALUE CONSIDERATIONS

In the book of Genesis, God revealed His sentiments about man:

> Then God Said, "Let Us make man in Our image, according to Our likeness; let them have dominion over the fish of the sea, over the birds of the air, and over the cattle, over all the earth and over every creeping thing that creeps on the earth." (Gen. 1:26)

It is worth noticing how this scripture verse establishes the value that God places on man, as a living soul created in His own image. Two distinct observations emerge from Genesis 1:26 which are relevant and crucial to our understanding of the believer's social-relational actions and inactions:

1. The fact that God resides in a unique three-person relationship—a tripartite association—that He, the Godhead, revealed by giving the command, "Let Us make man in Our image" (Gen. 1:26a).
2. The fact that God wants us to be a replica of Him, as well as the other two divine personages that constitute His total being—God the Son, and God the Holy Spirit.

God's intent for humankind—His creation—is therefore enshrined in the phrase "According to Our likeness" (Gen. 1:26a). His intent is for us humans to be like Him in all aspects of life. Consequently, I safely contend that it is God's desire to create and put into humans the values of His divine nature, including but not limited to norms, beliefs, ideals, and aspirations. In addition, God, in my opinion, purposed to empower humans who are His creation with a preexisting condition—a divine relationship—that He, the Godhead, forges with the other two divine personages of His being. Jesus made God's desire for this divine relationship evident when Philip asked Him to show them the Father:

Jesus said to him, "Have I been with you so long, and yet you have not known Me, Philip? He who has seen Me has seen the Father; so how can you say, Show us the Father? Do you not believe I am in the Father, and the Father in Me? The words that I speak to you I do not speak on My own authority; but the Father who dwells in Me does the works." (John 14:9–10)

Furthermore, a proclamation in the book of Psalms also underscores our relationship with the Father and goes to buttress God's divine intent: "I said, 'You are gods, and all of you are children of the Most High'" (Ps. 82:6). Therefore, God's intention to have a truly positive relationship and understanding with humankind measures up with the kind of relationship He has with the two other divine personages, the Son and the Holy Spirit.

In addition, value creation is paramount in the synthesis of life's products, not only at a spiritual level but also at physical, emotional, and social levels. Studio artists, for instance, are very sensitive to how they create value in their artifacts. A painter executes paintings admirably by way of controlling the physical, social, and emotional symbolisms of elements, objects, and subjects used in a given painting. Also, the amount of light or dark introduced into the elements within the painting partly determines the interest an observer would have in that particular painting. Similarly, a potter considers carefully the treatment and seasoning of the body of clay that goes into the production of pottery wares, even before passing them through the kiln or furnace, not to mention the color choices for the glaze and the varied degrees of color intensities to use.

As social beings, and believers we need to understand that a life that goes ungoverned by positive-value considerations is bound for failure, destruction, chaos, disorientation, or disintegration over time. We humans must seek relational considerations in one another that edify the soul and liberate the heart, spirit, and mind. Such an ideal would endear us to others, enabling them to feel comfortable in approaching us, converse with us, and enjoy our company. They would be more likely to join us in fellowship to the point of expressing themselves with absolute freedom of the heart, mind, and soul. I therefore argue, with a level of certainty, that the universe has lasted this long and still holds strong due to divine relational considerations that the Creator, God, factored into the creation process with delicate balance. Besides, the Creator of heaven and earth, including all things in the universe, places much value on each one of His creations.

In God's insightful and creative faculty, some products of His creation assume higher value levels than others. It is in such regard that the value placed on man exceeds any of God's other works of wonder, even though man is the last of His creations, as recorded in the creation story in Genesis 1. Man's ascribed value is made much more evident when Adam was assigned the duty of having dominion over everything on earth (Gen. 1:28–31), including all animals created by God. Adam's responsibility, which was to take care of and establish dominion over all of God's creations, increases man's value over other creations. It is worth noting, therefore, that in our attempt to take care of and establish domain, there is the central need for us to create an environment of respect for the fundamental dignity of all others over whom we have dominion. Respect for the dignity of all God's creation requires the exercising of positive relational-value considerations, be it toward man or beast. As parents, leaders, and heads of social groups, we owe it to God to ensure that the fundamental dignity and respect for all others is paramount in and outside our homes and families.

My dear reader, before you go any farther into reading this book, I would humbly entreat you to go through the activity below. Please be sincere when going through the activity. The benefit of knowing if this book has helped depends on how you conduct this initial activity. Thank you.

PRACTICAL ACTIVITY 1

To be performed in pairs

Please pair with someone in your immediate family whom you've seen all your life; or a friend or next-door neighbor with whom you have conversed for the past months or with whom you play and party, or pray, or work; or someone with whom you've met regularly on a one-on-one base or interacted with in, say, a neighborhood group.

Each of you should take a plain sheet of paper and pencil and follow the instructions for the activity below. You might ask what the need is for a practical activity before reading the book farther. Simply, this activity will give you an idea of how much you know about yourself and a person you have seen almost every day of your life. In addition, it shows your level of action or inaction in building relationships, the depth of your social engagements, and the extent to which you understand your paired partner from the time you first met until this moment of taking part in this activity. Please be aware that the exercise also marks the point at which you may determine, after diligently reading this book, if any change has occurred in you, such as:

1. The way you see yourself and perceive your siblings or other family members, friends, and neighbors
2. The way you think, act, and interact while in the company of others—friends, coworkers, neighbors, family members, or siblings
3. How your actions and inactions influence the way you think, create, and practice relational-value with those inside and outside your immediate or extended family and other social networks.

Now, to activity 1.

On the plain sheet of paper, you have in hand:

1. Write down any five acts of kindness which you may have seen your paired partner engage in, or in which you know your paired partner engaged.
2. Write down five different occasions when you saw your paired partner invite someone with a different skin color or accent into his or her house or apartment for dinner or a meal.
3. Exchange your activity papers.

4. Read aloud what your paired partner has written to see which of the five things written about you is true. Be honest.

5. Have a five-minute discussion on any of the facts written about you by asking questions and allowing your partner to answer candidly.

In this activity, you may decide to increase the number of things you write about each other's social-relational life, but you should not reduce the number. Also, if you are reading this book alone, rather than in a group setting, please take time to self-reflect on instructions 1 and 2. Try to ask yourself why your answers are possible or impossible. Were the actions of your own making or initiative? Did someone engineer or direct you to do them? Think along such lines.

Thank you, and enjoy.

SECTION 2
Relational-Value:
What (Is It)?

The term *value* may be ascribed different interpretations at any given point. I start this section by looking at four possible interpretations of the term and determining which of the four is appropriate for the discussion on creating and practicing relational-value. The four interpretations include the following:

1. *Value* may be interpreted as *anything deservingly held*; or the importance one assigns or gives to objects and subjects; or the usefulness of an animate or inanimate thing to an individual.

For instance, if I say, "The value of preparing myself for marriage cannot be overstated," I am simply using value to emphasize the *importance* of preparing for marriage. It also underscores the understanding of the urgency I may assign to preparations for marriage. Scripture says, "Do not fear therefore; you are of more value than many sparrows" (Matt. 10:31). By this scripture, we may arrive at the understanding that the value God places on His children is greater than anything else He has created. The statement further serves as a guarantee for our worth or importance to God, giving us a sense of pride (not arrogance) about the value He places on us as His creations. The statement brings with it a sense of comfort and security, knowing that God sees us and is always there for us. Therefore, those who honor Him in praises and fellowship are deserving in His sight.

2. *Value* can indicate the understanding one has about *the monetary worth of something*, whether animate or inanimate.

For example, if I say, "My house is valued at $190,000," or "My tithe each month is valued at 10 percent of my total monthly income," all I am suggesting is that the monetary worth of my house or the tithe I pay monthly in church is as such and nothing more. However, the monetary worth of things may alter as a result of an unforeseen change in circumstance; that is, the monetary worth of my house can change, becoming lower or higher, due to either deterioration or a renovation made to the structure. Similarly, though my tithe is valued at 10 percent, the monetary worth may change due to a demotion I suffered or a raise I received, which may lead to a lower or higher salary. One thing most evident is that while monetary worth can fluctuate, the value God placed on His children remains constant and never changes, as discussed previously with reference to Genesis 1:26.

3. *Value* also may be interpreted as an individual's *principles or standards that inform behavior*, or it could be an individual's judgment of what is important to him or her in life.

For example, we internalize our parents' rules and regulations, their actions and inactions, and they become our personal values later in life. Similarly, I may also internalize values through the reading and hearing of the Word of God and through parental instructions that may either be in line with learned godly principles or worldly practices acquired in life. Christian teachings, whether formal or informal, internalized through parental upbringing or the church, become standards that inform behavior. In other words, the actions and inactions taken in a family or on a Christian journey depend largely on acquired principles from the authority of our lives, which informs our behavior.

Behavior scientists or child psychologists, like Elizabeth Hurlock (1945), believe there exists a higher chance of children turning out to be wicked in later life when they are brought up in a home environment by parents with wicked tendencies. Conversely, a young child growing up in a loving and caring environment would learn and uphold the principles of loving and caring as he or she grows and becomes an adult. This viewpoint, I contend, may not hold true always, due to other unexpected factors that may change an individual's behavior toward another and his or her way of thinking about others. Yet it is true to say that, all other things being equal, the environment in which one is born sets the stage for social-relational values to be developed and retained.

4. *Value* may be defined in a fourth way by the visual or studio artist. The visual artist sees and defines value by assigning degrees of color, or chromatic intensity, such as a high degree of color intensity (vivid or light) or a low degree of color intensity (dull or dark).

For instance, a studio painter's simple method of changing the value of a color is to add the neutral white or black color to lighten or darken the original value. In doing so, that same action may raise or decrease the color's degree of intensity. On the other hand, one can also change the value of a color and its intensity by introducing that color's complementary into the mixture. Instead of using the neutrals black and white, one would use the complementary instead. A color's *complementary* is usually the color directly opposite the color in question on the color wheel or color circle. For example, red and green are opposite each other on the color-wheel, therefore they are complementary colors, so is yellow and violet, etc. To keep values rich and vibrant, it is always advisable to use the complimentary technique of mixing colors. Introducing neutral white or black into a color tends to reduce the vibrancy of the painter's canvas, and the color value and intensity will certainly change as well.

All four interpretations of value discussed, will be relevant to our discussions on relational-value creation in homes. However, the first, third, and fourth interpretations will be our main focus into our discussions moving forward. Besides, the third interpretation of the word *value* pretty much encompasses the first two interpretations.

UNDERSTANDING RELATIONAL VALUE

So far, we have established that an individual or group may consider a standard of behavior or judgment of what is important as *value*. Therefore, from this conventional understanding, I would personally define relational value as, "the degree of importance or intensity of purpose (in one's heart and mind), which influences our actions, inactions, and/or judgement of others," whether within or outside the family. So, how would you define relational value? I encourage you to come up with one, since it will help shape your understanding of discussions moving forward.

Relational value is largely sown, nursed, and nurtured to grow in the immediate home environment because the character or personality of an individual is mainly the product of the home. That is why we have the saying, "charity begins at home". Sound relational value acquisition must be in our thoughts constantly, expressed and acted out always by parents, caregivers, leaders, or people in authority. The kind of attitudes or behaviors we express in our interactions with others, particularly young children, greatly speaks to our internalized relational-value experience, either directly from the home or learned through teachings from secondary sources, such as peer groups and organizations, schools, community clubs, and churches.

More often than not, we do realize that some never had the luxury of growing up in a God-fearing and loving home. The raw worldly experience is all that we know and exhibit in new social settings. As a new entrant into a new social setting—home, school, club, or church— chances are, I may receive instructions based on the Holy Bible, that is, assuming the group values godly standards in its environment. Through such instruction, I may internalize principles of social living, as written in the holy scriptures. Also, it will refine and transform me to be much more socially adjusted and relatable, able to exhibit godly conduct toward others, such as benevolence, humility, kindness, and respect.

It is very important that we develop sound relational behavior in our homes because nothing is more important than the conduct we exhibit when we enter a secondary environment, where we interact with others previously unknown to us. In fact, positive godly values do determine the rate and extent to which we may win relationships, friendships, and ultimately, others into the body of Christ. On the other hand, negative behavior could deter friends and repel others from surrendering their lives to God. Let's ponder over the following questions for a moment:

- While interacting with your brothers and sisters at home or friends in school, college, or church, how do you see and view them?
- What kind of interest do you have in persons who randomly knocks at your door, or one you meet on the road with a problem but doesn't look like you, speak like you, eat what you eat, or dress like you?
- How do you accommodate a brother or sister or even a stranger who has offended you but does not look like you, let alone walk or act like you, share the same interests with you, work the same job or church ministry, or quote scripture as eloquently as you?
- What type of emotions emerge from the depths of your heart at first sight toward someone who does not speak your language or belong to the same social group or class, religious affiliation or work the same job as you?

Self-examination through questions like these may help us assess our current position in relational-value development, and the ways of God. It will help determine how we can (re)create and practice better relationships in the home and among others who are also God's people— His creations. It will help us perfect our relational barometers, such that they will be in synch with the values God wants His people to express among themselves. It is the nature of value I express towards another which could be measured as vivid or dull, high or low (Amagnoh 2014) from a pointillist perspective. That value is also dependent upon my assigned degree of intensity (Amagnoh 2014) or level of bias with which the value is expressed. (Assigned degree of value intensity will be fully discussed in Section 4 of this book.)

The holy scriptures remind us: "Judge not, that you be not judged" (Matt. 7:1). In fact, God knows how judgmental the human heart is and what humans are capable of inflicting upon one another. After all, He came and dwelled among us. He experienced our judgmental hearts firsthand. Therefore, knowing who we are, He cautions us, through His Word, against judging one another. Many other verses in scripture give us insight into what or how God wants us to behave towards one another, whether it's a brother, sister, father, mother, uncle, aunt, or a total stranger. For instance, the book of Matthew says, "Therefore, whatever you want men to do to you, do also to them, for this is the Law and the Prophets" (Matt. 7:12). Also, in the book of Proverbs, it is written, "A righteous man who falters before the wicked is like a murky spring and a polluted well" (Prov. 25:26).

In addition, the book of Ephesians states, "And have no fellowship with the unfruitful works of darkness, but rather expose them" (Eph. 5:11). Yes, you can expose them when you endeavor to be the light in the dark. These and many more scripture verses serve as a guide to our social and spiritual interactions with others. God wants the values I form in my heart and project toward others to be expressed through love and kind-heartedness, particularly, when it comes to showing others who He really is and what He stands for. In that manner, I may be better positioned to play my part by drawing the world onto God. As parents and leaders, we have an obligation not to cause anyone to lose the path to salvation and the hope of eternal life.

SECTION 3
Relational Value: *How* (Does It Happen)?

To create and practice relational value in a family does not happen out of the blue; it requires the interplay of a number of factors: first, understanding where those factors reside; second, how the factors manifest; and third, how they operate. These are critical to knowing how relational value may be created and practiced.

Values are usually picked up as we listen, talk, read, and perform roles in our homes. Adults are quick to correct the child when he or she goes wrong. The correction is always toward the ideals set by the authority figure, or the parent. A young child, doesn't have a say in creating personal values, unless such a child is on the streets; even then, some adults living on the streets may take the young street-child into their fold for guidance. Basically, the child still remains at the mercy of a higher authority even on the street, and the authority figure is ever willing to do whatever it takes to bend the child's will into submission and to conform.

DEVELOPING A FAMILY VALUE SYSTEM

The individual's social, spiritual, and emotional values are very much contingent upon the base values already in existence in the family. The reference to family, in this context, comprises the mother, father, and children, what the West refers to as the *nuclear family*. Individuals in every family constitute the basic unit upon which communities are formed. Within every family's primary environment, the individuals come together for activities and interactions, not to mention moments of worship for spiritual upliftment, usually under the leadership of the parents. The individuals who constitute that family or home environment then later enter a secondary environment, such as a school, community club, or church. The family therefore becomes the basic social block in that communal environment, while engaging in communal interactivities. After such activities, they go back to individual family homes, where social, physical, emotional, mental, and spiritual synergy or interactions continue.

Positive interactions, based on sound parental social-value principles, eventually mold the young child to become a by-product of a worthy home environment in the community. Besides, a peaceful, well-rested mind is usually in harmony with itself and others. Subsequently, developing a strong, desirable value system within our communities must begin from a home environment, devoid of psycho-emotional disturbances.

A strong, durable, and desirable relational value system, therefore, requires the interaction of two end domains. Simply defined, *end domains* are environments created by persons in authority to harbor, protect, educate, and train the individual or the social group. End domains are necessary requirements for establishing and driving specific social-relational value principles in an intended direction. They are operational, particularly in homes and within social organizations. They exist as two largely separate but interdependent types. These are:

- Relational end domain
- Institutional end domain

Relational end domain: Relational end domain deals with and develops the individual's character toward another or others in the family or community. Within this end domain, there exists other subdomains that determine the ultimate direction of the individual, in terms of character and social-relational values taught and learned. The parent or leader in the home is responsible for developing the personality and character of its individual members, who ultimately will become members of the larger society someday. A child's mental and emotional development comes by way of values upheld and practiced at a young age. Therefore, once grown, and as a product, he or she is first and foremost an individual brand; second, a finished brand of the family environment; and third, a family-brand-product intended for use in a larger community. Diagram 1 illustrates how the structures within the end domain operate in a family's life, for the greater good of society.

The relational end-domain segment of the diagram has four basic subdomains that operate individually and collectively to instill maximum relational value considerations in an individual. When any of the domain segments fail to establish in the consciousness of leaders in the home, the exercising of sound relational value becomes flawed at the child education and training level. Subsequently, it mushrooms to the larger community leading to a total disregard for basic human decency and dignity. In extreme cases, such a lack thereof, might even result in the loss of human lives. Jesus Christ mentioned with grave concern the lack of relational value among His people, the Israelites, in the book of Matthew, saying, "O Jerusalem, Jerusalem, the one who kills the prophets and stones those who are sent to her! How often I wanted to gather your children together, as a hen gathers her chicks under her wings, but you were not willing" (Matt. 22:37). This outcry, and fervent desire of the Lord, reveals the importance of relational value to God and for His people.

The four subdomains residing within the relational end domain are further complimented and firmly directed by the actions or inactions of other satellite domains, which include the family authorizing environment domain, the family spiritual environmental encounters domain, the pointillist-principle domain, the family value-end domain, and the family communication domain. Together, the pursuit and effective interplay of all these domains result in a family value production or reproduction worthy of commendation or otherwise. What a child learns within the relational end domain is ultimately carried into the larger community or society. Besides, the effective interplay of all subdomains in a family's life establishes the will of God and His agenda for His people on earth.

Institutional end domain: The institutional end domain deals with the secondary social organizations, groups, and clubs, with a mandate to instruct, uphold, and exercise specific values. While those values may be of corporate or organizational standards, they are mostly aided or compromised by the relation values the leadership brings to bear on the corporate values. The institutional end domain is also characterized by subdomains that determine the relational direction of the institution or organization, be it local, national, or international. (This type of end domain will not be discussed here but rather in a different volume.)

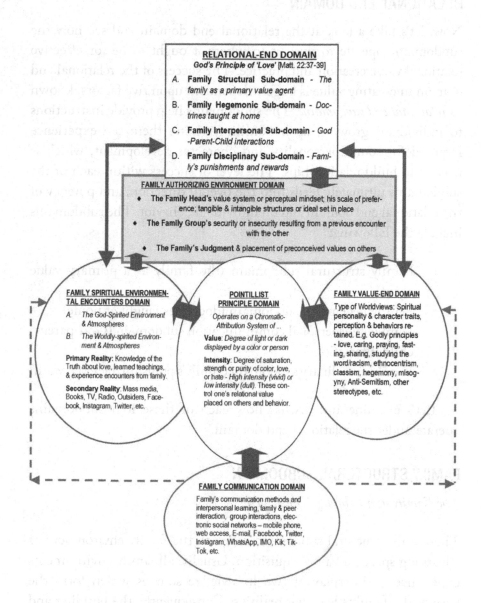

RELATIONAL-END DOMAIN
God's Principle of 'Love' [Matt. 22:37-39]

A. **Family Structural Sub-domain** - *The family as a primary value agent*

B. **Family Hegemonic Sub-domain** - *Doctrines taught at home*

C. **Family Interpersonal Sub-domain** - *God-Parent-Child interactions*

D. **Family Disciplinary Sub-domain** - *Family's punishments and rewards*

FAMILY AUTHORIZING ENVIRONMENT DOMAIN

♦ The **Family Head's** value system or perceptual mindset; his scale of preference; tangible & intangible structures or ideal set in place

♦ The **Family Group's** security or insecurity resulting from a previous encounter with the other

♦ The **Family's Judgment** & placement of preconceived values on others

FAMILY SPIRITUAL ENVIRONMENTAL ENCOUNTERS DOMAIN

A. *The God-Spirited Environment & Atmospheres*

B. *The Worldly-spirited Environment & Atmospheres*

Primary Reality: Knowledge of the Truth about love, learned teachings, & experience encounters from family.

Secondary Reality: Mass media, Books, TV, Radio, Outsiders, Facebook, Instagram, Twitter, etc.

POINTILLIST PRINCIPLE DOMAIN

Operates on a Chromatic-Attribution System of ...

Value: Degree of light or dark displayed by a color or person

Intensity: Degree of saturation, strength or purity of color, love, or hate - *High intensity (vivid)* or *low intensity (dull)*. These control one's relational value placed on others and behavior.

FAMILY VALUE-END DOMAIN

Type of Worldviews: Spiritual personality & character traits, perception & behaviors retained. E.g. Godly principles - love, caring, praying, fasting, sharing, studying the word/racism, ethnocentrism, classism, hegemony, misogyny, Anti-Semitism, other stereotypes, etc.

FAMILY COMMUNICATION DOMAIN

Family's communication methods and interpersonal learning, family & peer interaction, group interactions, electronic social networks – mobile phone, web access, E-mail, Facebook, Twitter, Instagram, WhatsApp, IMO, Kik, Tik-Tok, etc.

Diagram 1. Relational End Domain
Family Relational Value Creation and Practice Model
Source: Adapted and modified for social-relation
value education from Amagnoh (2014)

RELATIONAL END DOMAIN

Now, let's take a look at the relational end domain and see how the subdomains operate to push it to where it ought to be for effective relational value creation and practice. The success of the relational end domain in creating value is largely dependent upon five factors, known as *relational end subdomains*. The subdomains help provide instructions to individuals growing up in families, giving them the experience required for sound personality and character development, which is needed to build relationships. The level of success within each of the subdomains ultimately feeds into the overall direction, and potency of the relational end domain and on individual behavior. The subdomains include the following:

- Family structural subdomain (the family as a primary value agent)
- Family hegemonic subdomain (doctrines taught at home)
- Family interpersonal communication subdomain (God-parent-child interactions)
- Family disciplinary subdomain (family's punishment and reward)

Let's examine and discuss how each of these four subdomains operate under the relational end domain.

FAMILY STRUCTURAL SUBDOMAIN

The Family as a Primary Value Agent

The family structural subdomain refers to the family environment as a learning space for value acquisition. Usually, all family environments experience an interplay of two knowledge sources which form the base of the family's learning realities. Consequently, the building and learning of human relations in the family environment greatly depends on individual interactions with these two knowledge sources. That is,

1. Primary Knowledge Source
2. Secondary Knowledge Sources

Primary Knowledge Source: This knowledge source deals with self as a social being, learning within the home environment, an environment that is fully operational yet dependent on the capabilities and functionality of persons (parents, surrogates, or siblings) within the immediate environment. Primary knowledge is dependent upon realities that establish and encompass the extent to which the child's primary-knowledge provider is willing to assist, based on the primary-knowledge provider's own personal experience(s). In other words, a child's immediate family members are the primary agents by which and through which the child learns to communicate, socialize, and function effectively within and outside the home environment. However, the child's ability to function is limited by what the primary provider actually understands about creating and practicing sound relational values and what he or she is equally capable of offering the child through education and training.

Members of a child's immediate family consist of the mother, father, and siblings, if any. This group forms the child's primary social support system. It is the child's first point of contact with humans. Through the immediate family members, the child begins to internalize right and wrong, good and bad or evil, happiness or sadness, joy or pain, etc. He or she learns how to be kind or mean, how to love or hate, to be humble or prideful, to identify the desirable or the undesirable, to be benevolent or malevolent, to be charitable in giving or close-fisted, to feel another's pain or remain callous and indifferent, etc. The immediate family is an important group in determining the kind of person a young child will grow up to become. A child's self-identity, self-belief, emotional, physical, social, and mental developments are dependent on what the immediate family members have prepared for and are ready to offer.

In effect, the ability of the child to relate freely, speak, act, love, and respect the feelings of others depends greatly on the type and kind of people encountered in the immediate home environment, and right from conception. Behavior modeling by the mother, father, and siblings, as well as other adults, like grandparents, influences the child's learned and internalized actions, inactions, subjective and objective communication skills, and interactivity in life. Immediate family role models go a long way in influencing mental development and social-relational value acquisition. If child psychologists are generally of the view that children born in homes devoid of love and affection have a high chance of growing up to be wicked and unloving, then adults in charge of the child upbringing owe it to humanity to train and educate children with a substantial dose of love and affection. By such acts, adults would mold children into emotionally and mentally stable, desirable, and confident adults of tomorrow, who are grounded in the acts of building long-lasting relations and friendships with others.

I do not lose sight of the fact that not all parents or adults in charge of training children will model love and affection while performing their maternal and paternal duties in the home; it is impossible to give to another what you do not have. In fact, there are parents or adults who find absolute pleasure in the pain and discomfort they inflict on children. Therefore, adult trainers, educators, social workers, and all who are into the education and training of children need to uphold and engage kindness and love as top priorities in child-training and education. An otherwise false and outright misrepresentation of such relational values is bound to endanger the spiritual, social, psychological, and emotional development of the child.

Similarly, like a potter handling soft clay, parents and older siblings owe it to a young child to be sensitive to his or her mental and emotional needs by modeling positive interpersonal modes of behavior that the child sees and learns from. I would argue here that there is a flip side to positive role modeling that is much more dangerous to the child than cancer; that danger is a home environment full of hateful, angry, aggressive, and foul-mouthed individuals, whose model of behavior enables a young child to grow up as a product of those same antisocial standards. A life riddled with emotions of rage, wicked and callous tendencies are equally dangerous to family members, the immediate community, and all of humankind.

The holy scriptures warn us in the book of Proverbs: "Death and life is in the power of the tongue, and those who love it will eat its fruit" (Prov. 18:21). When it comes to the upbringing of a young child, it is important for parents and older siblings in the home to think about the kind of language used to address the child, whether it is by way of giving commands, engaging in discussions, or answering questions. The kind of action or inaction portrayed by adults in the home is bound to feed into the values the child exhibits in later life. Those actions or inactions may influence and determine the type of character the child may exhibit in his or her service to family, community, church, and country.

Let me sight an example to illustrate this point. I was born and raised in a Catholic home in Africa. Growing up, I never had access to the Holy Bible. I attended a Catholic primary and middle school and, later, a Catholic Secondary (high school) for boys. Until my entry into high school, I only heard the Bible read by the catechist when attending mass on Sundays. The Catholic catechism was the most common form of Christian literature available at home. Besides that, my Dad would buy me a novena pamphlet for my monthly twenty-one-day novena recitals in honor of the infant Jesus. Consequently, I never opened a complete Bible, featuring the Old and New Testaments, until I entered high school and started taking Bible Knowledge classes in the first year. The Knox version of the King James Bible was our textbook. And those Bible Knowledge classes were purely academic exercises, aimed at teaching the techniques required to answer questions in order to pass the final school certificate/General Certificate Examination (GCE), ordinary level examination.

Today, I look back with nostalgia and realize there wasn't a conscious effort by the early life education system to spiritually and relationally engage me through the written Word of God. The only need that was encouraged at all was to commit scriptural passages to memory for the sole benefit of passing an examination—an act we students at the time characterized as, "Chew, pour, pass, and forget." There was little, if anything, in those Bible study experiences that gave me life lessons in building relationships through God's Word.

Back at home, Dad was rarely around because he worked as a foreign service officer with the Ministry of Foreign Affairs. He was regularly on postings to foreign countries to serve on behalf of the government in those embassies. It meant there was considerable freedom with regard to the kind of actions or inactions I took on my own or the type of language I used to tell my jokes and make others laugh. In fact, adult control was rather minimal over my use of decent language and profanity, while conversing or telling jokes. Mom was only home on weekends. She was a teacher and would travel to another town to teach during the week. She would leave my sister and me in the custody of our aunt, travel early Monday mornings, and return late Friday evenings. Though Mom was very much against my use of vulgar words and gave me knocks whenever she heard such indecency from me, her constant absence did not help to stamp out that kind of behavior from my life. Besides, the urge to cut me slack outweighed how much she abhorred the vulgarity of my jokes. Having been through so much in her own life, those jokes kept the smiles and laughter on her face as well. She deplored the behavior in its entity, yet she could not condemn it. I grew up framing funny jokes and stories laden with disrespectful words and phrases.

I found joy in my jokes, simply because it brought laughter to my audience. Let me say I was a standup comedian of a sort. I labeled my jokes as stories from the *korkortiorkors notebooks*—the term 'korkortiorkors' I must say, is nothing other than a word we coined those days in high school to indicate a kind of mystery or magical nature of the diary from which we drew jokes. However, little did I know that such vulgarity, wrapped in and disguised by the cloak of entertainment, was never acceptable in the life of a Christian. I kept at it and continued for as long as the jokes gave my audience and me gratification. I was always the toast of most friends, boys and girls alike, as they enjoyed every bit of my company and laughed their heads off. I basked in their praises as they laughed their worries away, often with tears rolling down their cheeks.

My life, ladened with crudity in speech, continued until my late twenties, when I met a lady who drew my attention to the self-gratifying yet ungodly aspect of my being. She drew distinctions between healthy and unhealthy ways of speaking as a Christian. What's more, I always saw my challenges through a negative lens, while she had a positive attitude towards everything, with the understanding that God always is in control of every issue, no matter how difficult or challenging it might be. She told me that as a Christian I should always think and speak positively, into my own life, since life and death lay in the power of the tongue.

To this day, I still believe that meeting her was not just a coincidence. Her beauty restrained me in ways unimaginable. Her thoughtful personality and demeanor captured my heart then, and still does. Her words and sense of spirituality made me appreciate then that I needed to make a conscious effort to control aspects of my language and thoughts, as it could prove vital in keeping her longer in my company. And that was just what I did, as difficult as it was for me.

As fate would have it, she later became my wife and the mother of my three beautiful children. Our Bible discussion sessions were deeply meditative and inspiring. Gradually, she steered me away from using curse words in my jokes. She began to introduce me to the ways a good Christian must think, and speak to himself and to others. Eventually, she would be the one to lead me to the cross, as I surrendered my life to Jesus Christ, as my Lord and Savior. Interestingly, today I can hardly remember the numerous foul-mouthed jokes I stored as knowledge over those years. They have been replaced with words of hope, love, and encouragement for others, as I continue striving for absolute faith in my Lord, Jesus Christ.

I've described this experience to bring to light the fact that all actions or inactions, in the home or secondary environment, are critical in determining the knowledge base, character, and personality of a young child for life. If it happens that the child doesn't experience any other encounter, later in life, with an intensity strong enough to outweigh the primary experience stored through the initial encounter, he or she will remain with that primary experience and knowledge forever.

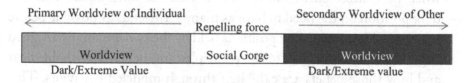

Diagram 2. Core Value Development
Source: Amagnoh (2014)

Secondary Knowledge Sources: These are sources from which knowledge is acquired, other than that taught at home by parents or surrogates. Secondary knowledge sources may complement or diverge from the action or inaction of the primary knowledge source. Secondary knowledge sources include the media—both audio and visual forms of communication, such as newspapers, radio, television, books—peer interactions, family friends, neighbors or outsiders, the school, community-organized groups and organizations, and social media platforms, including Facebook, Messenger, WhatsApp, Hangouts, Instagram, and Twitter and so on. An individual could acquire strong and sound relational values and attributes from his or her primary environment, but those primary values could clash with another he or she happens to meet in a secondary environment. It could also happen that such a clash might occur in the home environment between parent and son or daughter or between siblings. As illustrated in diagram 2, when the worldviews diverge, it creates a social chasm in which two individuals or groups repel each other as a result of their opposing beliefs.

In physics, we learn about a situation where objects with the same magnetic poles repel each other due to what is called repulsion. The principle of repulsion only holds true within the pointillist context when two persons with opposing values but with similar degrees of value intensity meet. Similarly, two strong and extremely dark value positions on opposite sides of the divide tend to repel each other, due to the opposing ideals or beliefs formed within their primary worldviews. For instance, a young man who comes from a family that believes in the principle of chastity and holds a strong, dark position on preserving himself for a future wife will have his relationship with another repelled when he realizes during an encounter that the other holds a strong, dark position on the need to have as many girlfriends as possible before marriage. The strong, dark positions held by the two are simply assigned degrees of value intensity to the principles and beliefs each holds dear and how those beliefs are exhibited through modeled behaviors. This individual belief system may also be explained simply as levels of bias, formed as a result of exposure to an environmental encounter(s), which is processed, stored, and becomes an indelible part of one's knowledge base.

FAMILY HEGEMONIC SUBDOMAIN

Doctrines Taught at Home

The family hegemonic subdomain is an important pillar to consider when looking at relational end domain within the home. The type and kind of social and ideological teachings handed down to the child by the parent will determine the social and mental path of that child toward self and others. The type of teachings with regard to class, social status, race relations, gender, etc., in the home environment become influencing factors in the thought patterns of the child. Thought patterns of self and of others—such as friends, neighbors, and those they meet later in life, in school, college, or other institutions of learning—are all influenced by what is carried from the home.

As the Bible instructs, "Train up a child in the way he should go, and when he is old, he will not depart from it" (Prov. 22:6). The kind of environment created and modeled by parents and older siblings, coupled with the way they speak of another and act or react toward others outside the family will determine whom the child will grow up to become, as well as the behavior he or she will exhibit toward others. Families need to consider questions such as:

- As a parent, how do you and your family view people with different skin colors than your own?
- As a parent or leader, are others outside your immediate family or group accepted or looked down upon?
- As a parent, and by your family standards, how do you view people from other races, ethnicities, or socio-economic groups which are not similar to yours? Do you see them as friends, neighbors, or human just like you; or are they people you deplore and consider to be takers, lazy, or nobodies?
- As a family head, have you ever broken bread with neighbors from different backgrounds—race, class, gender identity, or social group?
- As a parent, are you able to support others, both in private and in public, by standing up for those who do not look like you or talk like you?

Thinking about questions such as these will help us determine the type and kind of hegemonic or authoritarian environment we create and model for our children's mental, emotional, relational, social, and—above all—spiritual development.

Furthermore, within the young child's immediate family, upholding knowledge about truth is vital in value building. Besides studying and discussing scripture from the Holy Bible with our children, it is important to practice and model what we, as parents and surrogates, have learned from those biblical teachings so that the children may see and experience firsthand such positive values. Positive initial encounters are important in creating a healthy primary worldview for a young child. What the child sees, hears, learns, and does eventually becomes knowledge stored for future use.

For instance, let's imagine that during Bible studies, you taught your young child that the Christian faith does not encourage drinking alcohol, yet the child sees you coming home from work every Friday evening with a crate of beer in hand to feast on over the weekend. Or imagine reading scripture with your child that teaches him or her that God hates lies, yet when your landlord comes to collect the monthly rent money, you ask the child to answer the door and tell the landlord you are not home. Such deceitful signals can confuse the child. Besides, you are real in the child's mind and represent the primary authority and source of trust, the child will hold on to that trust, learn and internalize the behavior you are modeling over what the Word of God says. This is because parental actions or inactions are a young child's absolute reality.

When the child grows up and does not have an alternate experience—an encounter strong enough to overturn or outweigh what he or she has learned from you—those acts, words, or modeled behavior stay as the primary reality for life. Knowledge of the lies, the hate, and all behaviors contrary to the Word of God become indelible memories in his or her consciousness. The fraudulent acts are now and always will remain the child's primary reality that frames his or her worldview, until a new and powerful experience—hopefully—replaces the learned, sordid primary reality.

In other words, those deceitful experiences stored in memory as primary knowledge become the only glass through which the child will view and deal with members of the immediate environment and secondary sources, including neighbors, school and college friends, the church family, and the world at large. The child will go through life always living in a world outside the will and purpose of God for his or her life.

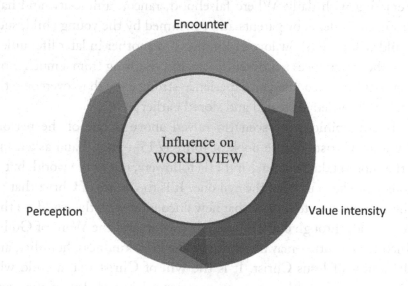

Diagram 3. (De)Constructing a Worldview
How Knowledge is Created and Stored in Individuals for Future Use
Source: Amagnoh (2014)

Diagram 3 illustrates how a worldview is created. For instance, when a young child is in the company of a parent, the child begins to assimilate all actions and inactions, verbal and nonverbal expressions coming from the parent. The parent's modeled behavior comes with an assigned degree of value intensity within the home environment. As the expressive behaviors become continuous in the life of the child, he or she will assimilate and internalize them, over time, as perceptions of the truth. The child then processes those truths, and stores them as knowledge, simply because of the trust he or she has in the parent, who models them. The stored knowledge then becomes the core foundation of the child's belief system, upon which his or her actions, inactions, and reactions will be based when dealing with others.

In other words, the child's stored knowledge is now his or her formed worldview or reality. That is why it is important to create a home environment and atmosphere laden with truths of love, kindness, humility, and selflessness, not falsehoods. Such truths, when experienced, form the knowledge base of the child we are training and interacting with daily. Where falsehood, rancor, animosity, and hate are values modeled by parents and consumed by the young child, such a child will never show love or kindness to another in later life, unless he or she experiences a different narrative, resulting from a much more intense future encounter, an experience strong enough to overcome the previous knowledge created and stored earlier in life.

In my opinion, the scenario raised above is one of the reasons why Jesus Christ—in the book of John 17:15—prayed and asked His Father not to take believers, and His followers, out of the world, but to protect and keep us from the evil one. It is the desire of Christ that we might be the ones to initiate that new encounter with the world, so that every child, through our Christlike behavior, and the Word of God—which is the truth—may be reborn in the love, kindness, humility, and selflessness of Jesus Christ. It is the will of Christ that a child who is in the world and has not yet experienced knowledge of the truth may come to understand the truth through the acts of His followers. Knowing the ultimate truth, through the actions and inactions of the believer and from the Word of God may become the new, intense encounter and experience; the new reality resulting from an encounter with the Holy Spirit that will help deconstruct the untruths of the past that reside as knowledge in the child's perceptive mind. The apostle Paul, whose former name was Saul, had a new intense encounter in the book of Acts 9:4; an experience which created a new reality, and a new knowledge which replaced the old, in his perceptive mind. The ultimate experience of encountering the Holy Spirit, therefore, will be lifechanging for a child. It is God's desire that through our actions, and inactions, others may come to know Him and the love He desires for us to share as neighbors.

FAMILY INTERPERSONAL SUBDOMAIN

God–Parent–Child Interactions

A family's interpersonal communication links the child to every other subdomain and involves a God-parent-child interaction; An interaction which may be examined through three relational modes. The modes are the following:

1. The God/Parent Relation and Interaction
2. The God/Child Relation and Interaction
3. The Parent/Child Relation and Interaction

Let's briefly discuss these three modes of relational interaction and see how they play into the relational value development of the child and, for that matter, the family.

God/Parent Relation and Interaction: God rules over the affairs of every family that offers Him the opportunity to do so. In my home, God is the supreme commander of my family, once I allowed Him. As a parent, I would have to play my role in all seriousness as God's representative. I am a representative of God, just like any ambassador would represent his or her country in another nation. I am the one who God has placed in charge of my family's affairs. Within that God/parent relationship, my portfolio of duties also demands a daily and constant reporting to God, the supreme commander. I am mandated to constantly communicate with my superior about the affairs within my jurisdiction, which is the home and my family that God has assigned to me. The daily spiritual reporting through interpersonal communication and fellowship with the Godhead is crucial to the success of my home and my family members. This is one of the reasons why the Holy Bible makes it clear in the book of James: "Draw near to God and He will draw near to you" (James 4:8a).

It is my responsibility as a parent, as it is for all parents, to report on the family's welfare and introduce every family member spiritually to the things of God by engaging in godly habits, such as reading and studying His Word, meditating upon the Word of God daily, fasting and praying, and seeking the face of God before undertaking any project, and in the midst of challenges. A parent's responsibility is to have a daily, constant conversation (in prayer) and fellowship with God. Such acts enable the Spirit of God to take control and direct all family affairs. It is also those moments of communing with God, studying, and understanding His nature, that helps in modeling the spiritual, mental, emotional, and psychological growth of the parent for onward transfer to the child, through training and behavior modeling.

I learned at a very early age to show kindness and to share, even in the face of scarcity. I still remember vividly the day when a strange woman walked into our house in Africa. I was eleven or twelve years old. She called my mother aside and engaged her in conversation for a while, in a voice almost inaudible. It was customary in African homes that the young ones were not allowed to be around adults when they were conversing. If they were, they had no right to interrupt. I watched as my mom listened attentively, and the woman poured out her heart, almost to the point of tears. Mom then called out to me and gave me instructions.

My mom (now deceased) was a teacher at the time, in the 1970s, and her salary was just about seventy shillings per month—the equivalent of about twelve cents today. Out of the seventy shillings each month, Mom would buy the following foodstuffs: a fifty-pound bag of rice; a twenty-five-pound bag of beans; one carton (ninety-six cans) each of canned milk, canned mackerel, and canned sardines, and a twenty-five-pound bag of granulated sugar. Buying these foodstuffs was a regular routine, month in and month out for her. My sister Matilda (now deceased) and I were her only two children left to feed out of the five children she birthed for our father.

Mom went through the agony of burying three of my siblings. I asked her one day why she would buy all that food every month when we were the only two of her children left. She answered: "Oh! My son, other people also need to have something to eat." At the time, it made little sense to me—until Mom called out to me after her discreet conversation with the strange woman. She told me to go into the bedroom, where she stored the foodstuffs with a bowl and measure out ten cigarette tins of rice. Then I was to look into each carton and take two cans each of milk, mackerel, and sardines and bring it to the woman. I complied with her instructions, and brought the bowl and its contents to her. I can still see the glow of joy on the woman's face, even after these years, as she thanked my mom and left. I then went to my mom and told her that the rice bag was almost empty, and what was remaining would not last a day. Mom simply looked into my eyes and replied, "Don't worry, my son. The Lord will provide." Today, I look back and draw the conclusion that those modeled moments of kindness and character did have an impact on the way I see and treat others in life.

I'm trying to show that a parent's most important duty is to establish God as the center of the family's daily life, around which everything else must revolve. Also, the parent must assist in leading the family to a personal spiritual fellowship with God. By doing so, he or she will fulfill, in the family's life, God's promise in Jeremiah: "Then you will call upon Me and go and pray to Me, and I will listen to you. And you will seek Me and find Me, when you search for Me, with all your heart" (Jer. 29:12–13).

As a parent, it's important to always remember that God is all-knowing, all-seeing, and all-present, yet He does not gate-crash into families or individual circumstances; He waits until he's invited, because He is a noble gentleman. The degree of interaction and fellowship a parent has at the spiritual level with God determines how He works in family or personal affairs. It is incumbent on us parents, to make time in seeking the face and wisdom of God, study the Word daily, meditate upon the Word, share and discuss the Word with our children.

As the head of the household, how do you see and discuss the family's challenges or circumstances? To what type of neighborhood fellowship do you belong and advocate for your home? What type of doctrines are taught in your neighborhood fellowship? Do those doctrines profess love and respect for fellow humans, from which the family can draw knowledge, or do they constantly teach hate, anger, and rage against others? How do you model the concept of love and respect for others, as an example for the child to emulate? Answering questions like these and many more and adjusting my ways to them will determine my spiritual relationship with God, and others, as well as my family's overall spiritual growth.

Parents, we ought to understand that having a relationship with God and a personal fellowship with God are two separate undertakings. They are never the same. Why is that so? Let me explain. Everyone living on Mother Earth has a relationship with God, simply because He created Adam. He breathed into Adam the breath of life, and Adam became a living being. From the rib bone of Adam, He created Eve, and together, both Adam and Eve became our forebears. We are creatures of God's creation. Besides, He allows the rain to fall and the sun to shine upon all of us without discrimination. He allows us to enjoy the air that we breathe for free, with no charges to anyone. From that angle, we all have a relationship with God, as our Father who provides for us, regardless of who we are and what we think about Him.

But the question remains: apart from the natural relationship we all have with God do we have a personal fellowship with Him? A personal fellowship with God requires a daily communication with Him—finding the time to speak with Him, studying His Word daily, and meditate upon His Word, while asking for deeper revelation and understanding into His Word, finding ways to reach out to the needy and the oppressed, in order to unveil His true nature. How we deal with our own personal fellowship with God will determine whether God's promise in Jeremiah 29:12-13 will be fulfilled in our lives.

Permit me to further illustrate this point. Those of us who grew up on farms or in towns and villages in the so-called third world, where farm animals moved around our dwellings all day long, may have observed the following example:

Throughout the time I lived in Africa, my mom always bred hens and cockerels, usually for the family's consumption on festive occasions, such as Christmas and Easter. Birthdays, whenever remembered, earned me, the celebrant, one boiled egg; the other children did not enjoy this privilege unless it was their turn to celebrate. Often, the hens would incubate their eggs, and they would hatch as many as ten or even fifteen chicks, depending on the fertility rate of the eggs.

By the way, hens that produce poorly by hatching only one, two, or three chicks were quickly "sent to the gallows" for not being viable, or sold in the market for cash. The newly hatched chicks and mother-hen were given limited freedom for about a week or two, until the chicks were strong enough to move around. The limitation of freedom for mother-hen and her chicks was achieved by restraining the mother-hen with a cord tied to one leg and the other end of the cord secured to a stick or stone in an enclosed area. This kept the chicks around mother-hen and prevented their straying away.

As the chicks were finally let out to feed in the open, one would notice always that a particular chick closely followed the mother-hen wherever she went, while the rest of the chicks did their own thing some distance away from the mother-hen. The chick that followed closely after the mother-hen always was rewarded with the thigh of a grasshopper, should the mother hen chase and kill one. The rest, who roamed about elsewhere in the distance, did not have that luxury of eating a grasshopper's juicy thigh. This observation has led to an old folk adage that says, "The chick that has concern and hangs out with the mother, seeking her welfare, is always rewarded with the juicy thigh of a grasshopper" (source unknown). This saying is often used to advice children who do not care about their parents, and it's also meant to deter children from misbehaving or becoming wayward.

Unfortunately, it's the chicks that wander far away from the protection of the mother-hen that get snatched by hungry hawks, which always lurk in the air, watching from above and seeking stray chicks to feed on. What happens is this: the chick always close to the mother-hen is heard instantly when it cries out to her, realizing imminent danger. The mother-hen, upon hearing the chick's outcry, rushes to its aid quickly, since it's near her. But the other chicks feeding far away from mother-hen, even when they cry out, she is unable to rescue them from the hawk, hence, they are snatched by talons and taken away.

This mother-hen/chick scenario exemplifies the difference between having a relationship with God, as opposed to having a personal fellowship with Him. All the chicks had a relationship with mother-hen, simply because she laid the eggs, incubated the eggs, and hatched them. All the chicks, from the time they were hatched, were protected and kept warm from the cold and sheltered from the rain—the mother-hen spread her wings to cover them. They all enjoyed that motherly protection by virtue of the natural mother-hen/chick relationship. But the chick who constantly followed (fellowshipping with) mother-hen closely had an added advantage in a time of crisis and was protected from hungry hawks.

As parents, we ought to use constant fellowship with God as a means to be thankful and to position ourselves for a rapid response from God in times of need. If we can have a personal fellowship, as well as a relationship, if we can seek Him with all our hearts and find Him, then we will call upon Him in times of trouble, and He will hear us and answer us. Remember that scripture says, "Draw near to God and He will draw near to you" (James 4:8a). As parents, we need to develop a personal fellowship with God and model that behavior, instead of going through life depending on just the relationship we and our families naturally have with Him. Let's make sure our personal fellowship with God serves as a fruitful lesson for our children to learn, internalize, and cherish for their own use, later in life.

The God/Child Relation and Interaction: This particular relational interaction is highly influenced by the spiritual standards set by the parent. As parents, it is our responsibility to set up a specific period during the day when the family studies God's Word together, even if for just a short time. A weekly Bible study time is also recommended when daily studies seem impossible. However, weekly studies shouldn't prevent us from encouraging the young child to read a verse from the holy scriptures every morning while meditating and discussing his or her thoughts with us about what was read. Once started and with time, the young child learns, through parental modeling, the act of assigning personal time to be alone in fellowship with God. By doing so, it becomes a normal routine for the child as he or she grows into a young adult. As the child cultivates this behavior at a tender age, he or she begins to see challenges and circumstances, personal or otherwise, through the lens of scripture. The young child's negative emotions and fears are held at bay through discussions based on what scripture says. His or her personal challenges and circumstances are surrendered to God, taking away fear and its psychological and emotional effects. Gradually, he or she totally surrenders heart, mind, and soul to the Holy Spirit and begins to sees everything through the prism of the holy scriptures. The child begins to understand at a tender age that seeking the face of God daily is not only for personal gain, but also an obligation to intercede on behalf of the family and friends, in light of what the Word of God says. So, at a young age, the child learns to talk with God, find time to study the Word of God, meditate on it and discuss the Word with the parents. And through parental guidance, the child sees and learns to perfect the one-on-one experience with God.

Once the child grows into a young adult, fellowship with others also increase, as social circles expand and spiritual groups become larger, accompanied by sharing learned habits from home through teamwork and discussions. Those spiritual group interactions in shared fellowship ultimately result in individual and communal breakthroughs, ensuing self-confidence, tolerance, the acceptance of others and by others, regardless of race, gender, social status, or religious creed. The concept of personal interaction and fellowship with God, learned from the home and based on love and respect for God and humanity, is transferred to others in a communal setting. It becomes a positive example from which others will learn and use in their own circumstances within the community.

The Parent/Child Relation and Interaction: Parental relations and interactions with a young child begin at the onset of conception. It is now understood in scientific circles that parents could start interacting with an unborn child at the prenatal stage of development, long before the child is delivered into the external environment. Studies by Partanen, Kujala, Tervaniemi, and Huotilainen indicate, "Extensive prenatal exposure to melody induces neural representations that last for several months" (Partanen et al 2003). This gives the indication that parents may start interacting with the child by talking, singing, and even reading short children's books and Bible stories while the child is still developing in the mother's womb. A congenial home environment, devoid of quarrels, vulgar verbal communications, and all forms of emotional and physical abuse, is required to give the child a good head start at the prenatal stage of development to enable the building of positive societal values. This kind of environment must continue as the child grows and learns how to talk through verbalizing and ultimately learning words toward language formation.

Cordial coexistence of both father and mother, in love and mutual respect for one another, is crucial. Exercising self-control throughout the child's formative years and beyond is necessary for the child's personal and interpersonal development. The ability of parents accepting their own mistakes by apologizing to each other when there is a misunderstanding, and to others and the child when the need arises is a valuable lesson. It may serve as a teachable moment, a hallmark of dignity and respect for fundamental values. Whatever principle of human dignity is upheld and modeled by parents in the presence of a child will ultimately reflect through behaviors that the child will exhibit outside the home, whether in the presence of neighbors, in school, college, or in other social group environments.

Children are said to be like sponges; they soak up anything within their environment. Even more, children are like computers. As the saying goes in the world of computers, "Garbage in, garbage out." Children give back to us exactly what we give them. When decency, respect, and love is modeled at home, the child will internalize such qualities and give back decency and love through language and behavior to the community. On the other hand, when cruelty, vulgarity, and disdain toward others are modeled, the child will learn and accept such qualities as the norm and give that back to society many times over.

Unfortunately, I cannot give love another, when I do not have love in me. I do not have love simply because I have never been shown love, or experienced what it means to love. Love is an interactive phenomenon, shown by words and through actions. The Bible says, "For God so loved the world that He gave His only begotten Son that whoever believes in Him should not perish but have everlasting life" (John 3:16). That single act of love was performed not only by God the Father, but also by His Son, Jesus Christ, whose inherent love also knows no bounds because He experienced it from the Father. Jesus knows what it means to show ultimate love by sending His own life to the cross in order to redeem a world in need of redemption and reconciliation onto His Father.

Sadly, if I had never been loved or experienced true love, chances are I might never be able to understand what Christ did for me on the cross; what it means to love by giving my all for the benefit of another; or give the ultimate love—*agape love*—knowing full well I would get *nothing* in return. Agape love is love given without seeking anything in return. It is given to a fellow human based on the conviction that God first loved me and gave His only Son to be sacrificed for my redemption from Adamic (or original) sin, which we all bear as a result of the disobedience of Adam to the commands of God in the book of Genesis. A replication of Agape love, by a friend, parent, teacher, leader, or surrogate to another, creates an immense sense of belonging in the individual to whom it is shown or given. Only parents and surrogates may teach a young child that kind of love, through Christ Jesus, who is the Word made flesh by the power of the Holy Spirit. Constant interactions with the child through the Word of God and the modeling of positive behaviors and attitudes, based on the Word, serves as the path for a child to live a life of affection and love for others; love which emulates that which Jesus Christ showed me by offering Himself as a sacrificial Lamb to atone for my sins and yours.

FAMILY DISCIPLINARY SUBDOMAIN

Family's Punishment and Reward

Punishments and rewards are critical disciplinary actions and very necessary components in the upbringing of a young child. A child's first source of discipline comes from the parents, as well as from the siblings, if there are any. An undisciplined life within the home and family is unacceptable to God because God is the *embodiment of discipline*. He dwells in and acts with discipline. Scripture reminds us, as parents and authority figures, "Spare the rod and spoil the child" (Prov. 13:24). An undisciplined home always results in anarchy and chaos. That is why it is important, as parents and as God's representatives, to raise our children with the utmost discipline required by the Word of God. Reward the child accordingly and punish him or her when need be. Punishment does not mean administering discipline with a heavy hand. It does not mean the projection of cruel and overbearing attitudes toward a defenseless child.

In fact, a disciplined punishment requires a delicate balance of corrective action with a considerable dose of love, in order to draw a child's attention to the misdeed and so he or she recognizes that the punishment was not given out of dislike but love. As parents, we ought to serve as counsel. Explain our position, and let the child understand the reason behind the punishment. Never punish a child without giving an explanation. Fathers and mothers, remember that your home is a microcosm of the larger community, so you cannot condone undisciplined and wrongful acts committed by the child in the home. Overlooking the child's undesirable behavior may send the wrong signal, indicating to the child that society *does* accept his or her actions or inactions. So, punish and reward where punishment or reward is due but with caution.

In my opinion, mothers are at the forefront as administrators of punishment and reward when it comes to child upbringing. They are the ones in contact with the young child twenty-four/seven, in most cases. Mothers carry pregnancies from conception through term and deliver when the baby is due. They have a unique opportunity to talk to their children, even when in the prenatal environment—the womb. When the child is born, the mother still has the lead command in controlling the child's discomforting patterns of behavior. Meanwhile, fathers and older siblings may play their initial roles as backup and support to the mother's disciplinary actions in the early stages of the child's development, until the child is weaned off breast milk in infancy.

Once the child is born, he or she is very much dependent on the mother. Every aspect of the child's survival and subsequent discipline in early life depends on what is permitted by the mother. Protection from bodily harm or injury, clothing, feeding, shelter, and acquisition of verbal skills depend mostly on the mother. The child's level of reliance on the mother is profound; therefore, it offers him or her no choice other than to totally surrender to the mother, regardless of the forms of punishments and rewards used. This is the reason why choices made as a mother can greatly enhance or endanger the child's life and subsequent behaviors expressed in larger society.

Let's look at how a mother's choices in performing a central task, such as feeding, may affect a child's level of discipline. In other words, a mother's feeding method can greatly influence a child's social behavior, habits, attitudes, and relational approach toward others.

Primary health care and postnatal care require that mothers feed their newborn children with milk directly from the breast, and exclusively, for at least the first six months after birth. This method of feeding is natural and God-approved in humans, but some women prefer to make other feeding choices rather than breastfeed exclusively for the required duration, for fear of losing the physical appearance of their breasts. A breastfeeding report released by the Center for Disease Control and Prevention (CDC) indicates that in the United States, "of approximately 4 million babies born in 2015, most (83.2 percent) started out breastfeeding – but many stop earlier than recommended" (CDC 2018).

The report further indicates that "good nutrition starts with breastfeeding exclusively (only breast milk) for about the first six months of life, as recommended by the American Academy of Pediatrics' Policy on breastfeeding. While nearly 6 in 10 (57.6 percent) infants are still breastfeeding at 6 months of age, only 1 in 4 are breastfeeding exclusively." What's more, the report spells out the benefits of exclusive breastfeeding which includes, "reduced risks of asthma, obesity, type 2 diabetes, ear and respiratory infections, and sudden infant death syndrome (SIDS). Breastfeeding can also help lower mother's risk of hypertension, type 2 diabetes, and ovarian and breast cancer" (CDC 2018). Yet, most mothers see exclusive breastfeeding as a personal threat.

My conversations and interactions with women over the years reveals that some mothers are overly concerned about their breasts losing form or becoming saggy and flabby. They are anxious about the fact that their breasts will no longer have the turgid, bouncy, and buoyant appearance that would instantly turn a man on. The fear of losing the youthful physical appearance of the breast causes some to throw caution to the wind and to choose bottle feeding over exclusive breastfeeding. Such a choice, besides endangering the child's overall health, may prove damaging to the acquisition of desired social behavior. This is because a feeding bottle is lifeless and cannot respond to external stimuli whether pleasant or painful, desirable or undesirable.

The point is, during bottle feeding, when a baby presses an itchy gum or teeth on the rubber nipple of the feeding bottle, there is no opposite reaction to signal to the child that what he or she just did was wrong.

As such, the child goes through early life, feeding on milk, mastering and perfecting how to bite on rubber nipples. This act—biting on the rubber-nipple of a feeding bottle—greatly affects the child's mental and social development, since it's performed without consequences. The child then grows with a false notion or belief that biting is good and feels good, and biting does not attract consequences. Such a habit gone unpunished might eventually lead to cannibalism in the child, with the possibility of biting siblings or the mother, at the least opportunity, or bite classmates in school, with or without provocation.

Alternatively, when a mother breastfeeds her child, a bond is generated through the breastfeeding process as mother and child constantly gaze into each other's eyes. A bond of love, affection, admiration, and sincerity of heart toward each other becomes evident with time. Now, it comes to the point where the baby wishes to calm the constant itching of the gum by pressing the gum or teeth on the mother's nipples. The mother then reacts immediately to the painful stimulus, usually by withdrawing her nipple from the baby's mouth. As this action/reaction scenario continues during breastfeeding sessions, the baby begins to internalize the fact that any time he or she presses gum or teeth on mommy's nipple, mommy withdraws nipple, and milk doesn't flow anymore.

Over time, the child learns through experience that biting keeps away good things like milk. The experience is stored as knowledge, and he or she will never bite the mother again during breastfeeding sessions, let alone others. Such a child would begin schooling or enter the larger society, knowing that biting is not a good idea. Hence, the child will not attempt to bite others. Also, breastfeeding has an added advantage besides bonding and the control of cannibalism in a child. It allows the mother to identify, at an early stage, any dangerous emotion, such as anger, aggression, sadism, and so forth. So, breastfeeding presents the opportunity to change hostile emotional behavior before it becomes a major attribute of a child's basic instincts and character.

Parents and older siblings in the young child's life must understand that as the child starts school, his or her social network will expand through interactions at school and in other public spaces. The child will begin to question differences in dealing with everyday subjects, such as giving, sharing, rewards, and punishments. In fact, the child may get confused when he or she shares with a friend the answer to a mathematics problem during an examination and then gets punished. It is the obligation of the home environment to let the child understand that while sharing is a healthy human and Christian character trait, some kinds of sharing can get one in trouble, such as sharing your answers with others during an examination in school. Let the child understand that while Christ encourages us to share our blessings with our neighbors, it is not a good idea to share or keep things that societal law prohibits.

In fact, there are many verses in the Bible that encourage us to give and share with others. It is the desire of God for us to give in response to the grace He renews in our lives every morning. For instance, in the book of Hebrews 13:16, scripture encourages us saying, "But, do not forget to do good and to share, for with such sacrifices God is well pleased." Also, in the book of Deuteronomy 15:7-8 it is written: "If there is among you a poor man of your brethren, within any of the gates in your land which the LORD your God is giving you, you shall not harden your heart nor shut your hand from your poor brother, but you shall open your hand wide to him and willingly lend him sufficient for his needs, whatever he needs." Furthermore, Deuteronomy 15:10 says, "You shall surely give to him, and your heart shall not be grieved when you give to him, because for this thing the LORD your God will bless you in all your works and in all to which you put your hand." While goodness and blessing come out of giving and sharing, it's important to remind the child that it's wrong to share something that he or she knows can bring trouble to a friend or neighbor. Let the child understand that to be a valuable and good friend, it's always good to put the interest of friends and others above self.

The idea of placing others first is what Jesus came to teach us. God demonstrated His love for us by putting us first, thus offering His Son as a sacrifice for the atonement of our sins. This measure of love is recorded in the book of Romans: "But God demonstrates His own love towards us, in that while we were still sinners, Christ died for us" (Rom. 5:8). Similarly, in 2 Corinthians, this ideal is again made known, when apostle Paul writes, "For He made Him who knew no sin to be sin for us, that we might become the righteousness of God in Him" (2 Cor. 5:21). Such is the act which, when modeled at home, teaches the young child to put others first.

SPIRITUAL ENVIRONMENTAL ENCOUNTERS

In discussing how value is created within the relational end domain, one must not lose sight of the environment where our relationships are cultivated and strengthened. It is critical to identify and uphold the right environment, whether at home, school, college, church, or in any social or corporate organization, for the attainment of a sound value system.

As human beings, we need to understand that we are all created equal. Apart from Adam and Eve, who, in Genesis, were personally formed by God, the rest of us exist through God's purpose for humanity. He said, "Be fruitful and multiply; fill the earth and subdue it" (Gen. 1:28). Therefore, in line with the sacred order of procreation, conception in a human is always the result of a union between a male sperm and a female egg. It does not matter whether conception occurred as a cross between a mixed race of black and brown, white and brown, or cherry and cream couples or between same-race parents. Every human is the product of a sacred union—a male spermatozoon and a female egg. This basic fact means that everyone on earth was born equal.

However, the environment into which one is born and bred sets a perfect stage for the eventual disparities we see in our values that are learned, carried along, and shared and practiced well into adulthood. Our norms, aspirations, culture, arts, music, and language are all environmentally controlled. Hence, we are all products and by-products of our environmentally induced and learned experiences. The environment controls and determines our personalities and characters—who we are individually and the kind of human being we grow up to become. Therefore, when it comes to the relationships we build with others, the environment of growth plays a significant role.

THE RIGHT ENVIRONMENT AND CHOICE OPTIONS

Parents and those in leadership positions need to understand that the phrase *right environment* is relative and highly subjective. It is subjective because the values to which a parent or leader ascribes and instills in members within the environment of authority has to be first made teachable through the parent's personal beliefs or principles. That is, the internalized attitudes and norms upheld by the parents or leader determine the home environment.

When the parent is convinced about a particular principle, such a valued conviction will rule throughout the home (primary environment). It is parents, guardians, or family heads who decide the kind of environment they want their children (or members) to grow up in. Once decided, daily training, teachings, and instructions are tailored to match up with their belief systems. All character modeling is performed based on the parents' valued convictions. The same is true of leaders in organizations, whether social, corporate, or religious.

As parents, we must know that personal beliefs control the making of choices, and choice options are necessary because of our daily encounters. Even more, our choices depend on and are controlled by the *principle of dualism*. That is, there are two sides to every coin, and at every turn in life, we are faced with the need to make a choice. The ultimate choice we make is a *desired choice*. Every desired choice triggers a consequence. While the consequence of some choices may be short-lived, others last for a lifetime and beyond. In other words, any choice we make today, as parents, has the capacity to present us and our offspring with consequences for generations to come.

The principle of dualism may also present itself to us by way of emotions and moods we accept and show daily, such as joy and misery, love and hate, benevolence and malevolence, greed and generosity, happiness and sadness, anger and pleasantry, pride and humility, aggression and meekness, pain and comfort, jealousy and gladness, or laughter and weeping. Every turn on life's journey demands making a choice. Ecclesiastes 3:1–8 talks about the idea of dualism as seasons or spaces in time. The environment we live in will always throw the dualistic principle at us, and at will, since we do not live in the environment alone.

For me to be able to control, ignore, accept, overcome, or make the right choices at any given time is a matter of the attitude and the personality I have developed over time. The choices I make, therefore, are heavily dependent on the instructions I received and kept, habits I formed, and skills I learned within the experience of the home environment—my initial environment of social, mental, and emotional empowerment. Consequently, my choices will constantly bring into question the type and kind of environment to which I was exposed while growing up.

Another agent that influences the home environment is the secondary reality that exists around and within the home. In other words, as a parent or leader in the home, the kind of friends with whom I associate and fellowship or those I allow to come near my family members is my secondary reality, which will greatly influence activities within my home environment. Understanding the forms of secondary information that I allow and encourage the children to bring or access at home is crucial to their social development. Apart from siblings at home, what kind of personalities in the neighborhood is my child socializing with? Who are my child's friends, and what are they like—spiritually, emotionally, mentally, and socially—in their homes? What do they enjoy doing as a hobby? What type of jargon or words do they use, and how decent are those? Are the lifestyles of my family's secondary associates relevant to the social and spiritual needs of my family? Examining these questions and more would go a long way toward determining the relational, and spiritual character of my home environment, as well as the environment I am creating for my children to grow up in.

Parents and older siblings have an obligation to introduce and expose the child to positive secondary realities outside of the home environment. It is a parental duty to guide little minds in the right direction. Dealing with the right secondary realities and associations will help jump-start an understanding of positive social relational-value forms.

It is important to note that my child's test of character in making choices is not best tested when I am around, or he or she is in the learning process, but rather in my absence or the absence of the authority figure.

It means in a home environment, critical choice-making is well verified in moments where the child/trainee is faced with making a choice alone in the absence of the parents. As a learner and a trainee under our parents' authority, what desired choices do we make when they are not looking or are not physically present at home? Are those choices in line with what they have taught us in reference to the Word of God, or do we make choices based on how we feel in the moment—the here and now? In most cases, the latter option may go contrary to the Word of God, as we often respond to the desires of the flesh when we do not stop to think through our choice.

Children grounded in the Word do know that in the physical absence of parents, there is a stronger spiritual presence with us—God the Father—just as Moses instructs, "And the LORD, He is the one who goes before you. He will be with you; He will not leave you nor forsake you" (Deut. 31:8). Our desired choices must always be in line with God's Word and His will for us. We must always be guided by the understanding that when an authority figure is absent there is always someone greater watching us, and that is God—the all-seeing, all-knowing, and ever-present God.

Parents and children, understand that acting outside God's instructions, and His Word, may lead to devastating social and spiritual outcomes for our future—outcomes that may affect our families and offspring for generations to come. For instance, in the book of Genesis 3:1–6, Eve made a preferred choice by taking Satan's word over God's divine instruction, given to her through Adam. In Adam's absence, she made a choice contrary to God's instruction. Similarly, Adam, presented with the story of the fruit, as told by Satan through Eve, also made a choice. It was a desired choice. And his choice was made to satisfy a woman, rather than keeping with the divine instruction of God. Adam's momentary lapse of mind in making that desired choice ultimately led to God's pronouncements in Genesis 3:14–19, with consequences that would last for generations to come.

HOME ENVIRONMENTS AND ATMOSPHERES

Every parent or family head has the option to choose the environment which will be conducive for educating and training the child in order to attain his or her God-given potential. Parents have the option to choose one of two types of home environments:

1. God-spirited home environment
2. Worldly, flesh-driven home environment

Within each of the two types exists various kinds of atmospheres that condition the environment in which the home will operate. Atmospheres change and regulate the values, principles, actions, and inaction which function in any given environment. In other words, the chosen environment exerts its influence on members through the kind of atmospheres it generates to ultimately moderate the character and behavior of members of that environment. It is the existing regulatory atmospheres that mold the character and attitudes of individual members—the life one chooses to lead and what to become.

Before I go any further, it is important to remember that the terms *type* and *kind* do not mean the same thing. While *type* may refer to classifications of a sort, *kind* grants us the knowledge of specifications under the classified type. In other words, one may want to state the kinds of objects that may exist under a particular classified type which give that type its basic function or character. For example, an alcoholic beverage is a type of drink laden with alcohol content; once ingested, it is capable of sending an individual into a state of slumber, stupor, insobriety, and disorientation. On the other hand, a nonalcoholic beverage is a type of drink with no alcohol content. These two types of beverages exist as the extreme opposite ends of the beverage continuum, and they have specific brands or kinds falling under their type classification. Therefore, looking at alcoholic beverages as a type, one may find different kinds, such as Beer, Whisky, Rum, Gin, etc., with different levels of alcohol concentrations. Similarly, we may find different kinds of nonalcoholic type beverages on market shelves with brand names such as: Fanta, Sprite, Pepsi-Cola, Crush, Coca-Cola, etc., with varied levels of sweetness.

Let's take the explanation of the terms *type* and *kind* further into the world of art. The textile designer, in composing a design for a textile piece may uses lines. He or she has the option to choose or combine three category-type of lines available to the textile artist:

1. Natural lines
2. Artificial lines
3. Accidental lines

Each category-type of lines has kinds of lines that fall under it. For example, under the first category-type, *natural lines*, one may see kinds of lines such as: a strand of hair, limbs of mammals, human fingers, creeping and climbing vines, tree branches and stems, lightening, a quill of a bird, animal intestines, spider-webs, cucumber, carrots, etc. These objects fall under natural lines as a category-type because they represent naturally existing forms, whose basic structure could be represented using a line with varying degrees of character. The second category-type, *artificial lines*, are manmade or manufactured. Different kinds of manmade line exist, such as electric, telephone, and cable wires (of varying thicknesses), woven ropes and cords, sewing threads, roads, streets, pathways, hunter's trails, sellotapes, and tape measures, etc. The last category-type, *accidental lines*, are lines which occur or are created unintentionally. They may result through actions from nature, human errors or mistakes. The kinds may include, stains from spilled or splattered milk, or blood, or water, or ink, a crack in a mirror, or glass, cup, or rock, etc. Such line patterns, once created, cannot be recreated through a repeated action to achieve the exact qualities or characteristics as the first. An attempt to recreate by repeating the action would result in a different outcome altogether, hence the term, *accidental*.

So, now that we know the difference between type and kind, let's take a look at the two types of environments and the kinds of atmospheres that may exist within each of these environments.

THE GOD-SPIRITED HOME ENVIRONMENT

A God-spirited home environment is an environment in which the parents invite and allow God to rule and control the affairs of the home through the power of the Holy Spirit. This type of environment exists first in the heart, soul, and mind of the parent, who is a vessel through which the Holy Spirit will operate and extend outwardly to the children, neighbors, and beyond.

A God-spirited home environment starts with the parent first inviting God into his or her heart, where the breath and Spirit of God resides, once invited in. The Spirit then works from the inside out, taking up the whole body—which is the temple of God. This position is reinforced in apostle Paul's first letter to the Corinthians, in which he affirms, "Do you not know that you are the temple of God and that the Spirit of God dwells in you? If anyone defiles the temple of God, God will destroy him. For the temple of God is holy, which temple you are" (1 Cor. 3:16–17). Paul further drives home the issue of the body as God's temple by explaining:

> Do you not know that your bodies are members of Christ? Shall I then take the members of Christ and make them members of a harlot? Certainly not! Or do you not know that he who is joined to a harlot is one body with her? For "the two," He says, "shall become one flesh." But he who is joined to the Lord is one spirit with Him. Flee sexual immorality. Every sin that a man does is outside the body, but he who commits sexual immorality sins against his own body. Or do you not know that your body is the temple of the Holy Spirit who is in you, whom you have from God, and you are not you own? For you were bought at a price; therefore, glorify God in your body and in your spirit, which are God's. (1 Cor. 6:15–20)

The moment I accept Christ Jesus as Lord and Savior and am baptized by immersion in water, I receive the in-filling of the Holy Spirit. I become a new person—a believer and follower of Christ.

Apostle Paul puts it this way: "Therefore, if anyone is in Christ, he is a new creation; old things have passed away; behold, all things have become new" (2 Cor. 5:17). A new environment is created in my heart through Christ Jesus, as my old person no longer exists. The Holy Spirit takes over the new me in Christ Jesus. I begin a new life, living in Christ, and Christ living in me. The presence of the Holy Spirit becomes stronger and stronger with time in this new godly environment inside of me. The strength of the Holy Spirit becomes greater in me as I continue to create and observe godly atmospheres—the hallmark of my new life in Christ Jesus. Once that inner self is made new with the presence of a godly environment, a spiritual and physical transformation will occur in me. Such a transformation has a ripple effect on the surrounding environment, such that I feel and see a change in my actions and inactions, my mode of behavior, and my character toward others. My worldly ways no longer appeal to me, giving way to a new spirit-filled me, grounded with belief in Christ Jesus.

Atmospheres in a God-Spirited Environment: In every God-spirited environment, there exists kinds of atmospheres. Atmospheres may be described as simply characters, attitudes, and daily habits or practices that I perform in my environment which go to show what I believe in, and what my environment represents. A God-spirited environment has certain habits and practices that describe the character of the environment. These include the atmosphere of belief in Christ as the Son of God, the atmosphere of fasting and prayers, the atmosphere of seeding and giving, the atmosphere of studying God's Word, the atmosphere of meditation and fellowship, and the atmosphere of evangelism. Others include the atmosphere of love and compassion, the atmosphere of hope, the atmosphere of faith, the atmosphere of forgiveness, the atmosphere of honesty and humility, and the atmosphere of respect among others.

We must remember that a God-spirited environment and its atmospheres does not exclude the family from temptations and trials. In fact, trials and temptations, long-suffering, and persecution are, in themselves, atmospheres that God-spirited environments endure as a testament of faith in God. The choices I make when faced with the atmospheres of adversity attest to my belief or unbelief in God. Godly atmospheres, once summoned, will influence and transform a family's perception, character, practices, and attitudes toward themselves and others around them. A family environment with belief and ascription to the atmospheres outlined above is no doubt a God-spirited environment, availing itself to the service of others and God.

God-spirited atmospheres drive what parents desire to learn and teach themselves through the reading and studying of God's Word and its interpretation. Such understanding comes through revelation and insight by the power of the Holy Spirit. Immersing oneself in God-spirited atmospheres empowers an individual to abstain from ungodly practices and behaviors, such as alcoholism, adultery, fornication, backbiting, gossiping, and all forms of malevolence against family members and neighbors. Establishing God-spirited atmospheres allows the creation of positive encounters for each member to experience within that family environment. Each God-spirited atmosphere, once experienced, enhances behaviors in positive and Christlike ways, teaching and exposing others within and outside the God-spirited environment. In addition, God-spirited atmospheres, once adopted, ensure education and practices of sound social relationships, such that it becomes an integral part of the child's psyche for use within and outside of the home and family environment.

THE WORLDLY FLESH-DRIVEN ENVIRONMENT

Biblical accounts document the fall of Lucifer, also known as Satan, and his fellow rebel angels who revolted against God. It was a rebellion that led to God casting Lucifer and his followers out of heaven onto earth. Scripture warns us about the intentions of Satan here on earth: "Be sober, be vigilant; because your adversary the devil walks about like a roaring lion, seeking whom he may devour" (1 Peter 5:8).

Satan roams this earth with one intention: to create his own earthly power and kingdom as an alternative to God's heavenly kingdom. His aim is to disrupt God's intent for His children. Therefore, in order to achieve his disruptive plan, Lucifer creates and presents an alternate environment full of falsehoods, which seeks to draw the unsuspecting person or child of God away from God's purpose and plan for His children. Lucifer's alternate environment capitalizes on the frailty or weakness of the human mind and our constant craving to satisfy fleshly desires. This feebleness of mind and yearning to satisfy fleshly desires was first seen during Eve's encounter with the serpent in the Garden of Eden—Gen. 3:1-7.

The worldly flesh-driven environment I may describe simply as, "an alternate spiritual environment that is created by Satan, controlled, and governed through lies to undermine God and His will for humankind." This worldly flesh-driven environment offers quick forthcoming opportunities to humans—God's creation. Sadly, the individual's readiness and desire for earthly possessions and riches helps drive and expedite Satan's agenda. The book of Matthew exhorts us against Satan's diabolic intentions: "Do not layup yourselves treasures on earth, where moth and rust destroy and where thieves break in and steal; but lay up for yourselves treasures in heaven, where moth nor rust destroys and where thieves do not break in and steal" (Matt. 6:19–20). In other words, activities that occur in a worldly flesh-driven environment are temporal, running hostile to the written Word of God.

Atmospheres in a Worldly Flesh-Driven Environment: Unlike a God-spirited environment, a worldly flesh-driven environment creates atmospheres that give members a feel-good mentality and appreciation of life. Marked by deceitful imitations of God's goodness, these atmospheres offer false niceties—proposals of remarkably spectacular rewards for anyone who will obey and stay obedient by simply bowing to Satan as lord.

Unfortunately, the rewards promised within these atmospheres are short-lived and come at a great cost to members. The atmospheres created in a worldly flesh-driven environment are usually extremely appealing, particularly to the unsuspecting individual and all those willing to throw caution to the wind. The Bible contrasts these atmospheres by comparing it to pathways in the Christian-walk of life: "Enter by the narrow gate; for wide is the gate and broad is the way that leads to destruction ... Because narrow is the gate and difficult is the way which leads to life, and there are few who find it" (Matt. 7:13-14). By this comparison, the Bible deliberately attempts to dissuade, caution, and direct humanity onto the right path—enduring the will and purpose of God.

Activities within worldly flesh-driven atmospheres are almost always described as, "fun." Those who comply with this environment are never satisfied, physically or mentally. Members become spiritually dead, with a blunt conscience toward the Word and things of God. They are uncontrollably addicted to deception and deceit which characterize these atmospheres, with practically no freedom from outright manipulation by Satan and his cohorts.

It is very difficult for anyone, once caught up in its control, to recognize and subdue the clutches of a worldly flesh-driven environment and its enabling atmospheres. Most often, we see and refer to the addictive behavior within the worldly atmosphere as *lust*. Some of the daily or frequent habits which members may engage in include, the atmosphere of alcoholism and smoking, gambling, womanizing, idolatry, veneration, adultery, fornication, and pornography. Others are the atmosphere of sex trafficking, incest, lying, and sodomy. The rest include the atmosphere of greed of all kinds—for money, power, and so on. These atmospheres absolutely take over the psyche of members, overpowering, corrupting, and eroding their hearts and conscience—God's Spirit-presence—with deliberate precision.

Each of the atmospheres within this environment may lead individuals into a state of ecstasy, elation, joy—you name it. At some point, the person interprets the false physical and emotional rewards of the environment as pure luck, or believes destiny has smiled upon him or her. Performers within a worldly flesh-driven atmosphere hold on to a self-gratifying narrative which results in a false conclusion: "Finally! I have arrived."

The temptation story in the book of Matthew 4:1–11 exemplifies how Satan uses the atmosphere of false niceties to generate interest and lure the individual or the believer. In this biblical account, Christ Himself encountered Satan after fasting for forty days and forty nights in the wilderness. The inherent message of this account suggests that a worldly flesh-driven environment and its accompanying atmospheres are real. It is Satan's well-orchestrated plan not only against believers but against all of humanity. It again suggests that such ungodly environment and its atmospheres, as well as the accompanying promises, are unavoidable for as long as we live in this mortal world in which Satan rules. Nonetheless, the question we need to ask ourselves is, who is most pressured to become vulnerable? Is it the believer or unbeliever?

Regardless, it is evident from the temptation account that when I gravitate toward an intense fellowship and worship of God, with an added value of creating an atmosphere of fasting and prayers, Satan's aggressiveness to dislodge my trust in God intensifies. Satan then plans to deploy very trick and atmosphere, to lure me away from God's purpose and plan and into his fold. This notwithstanding, I can overcome any worldly flesh-driven environment and atmospheres by constantly applying God's Word to any challenging environment and its false atmospheres, just as Christ did, and He encourages us to do same through a number of scripture verses:

> You are of God, little children, and have overcome them, because He who is in you is greater than he who is in the world. (1 John 4:4)

> For whatever is born of God overcomes the world. And this is the victory that has overcome the world—our faith. (1 John 5:4)

> These things I have spoken to you, that in Me you may have peace. In the world you will have tribulation; but be of good cheer, I have overcome the world. (John 16:33)

Many more such verses encourage us.

We parents, educators, trainers, and instructors need to make this knowledge of the power of the Word of God known to our children and all those who come under our authority to be educated, and guided by the truth. Besides, it demands that we hand down—through our instruction and modeling the practical constructs of good morals over evil—God's love over Satan's hatred. We parents must endeavor to create a godly environment and awareness for our children to grow up in and flourish, for the greater good of all humankind.

SECTION 4
Relational Value: *When* (Should It Be Practiced)?

A family's perceptual development—its production and reproduction—are relevant to the building of relationships and value creation. A child's view of another is a direct result of the type and kind of instruction, training, education, and modeled behavior that he or she has been exposed to in the home, through parents, adults, or family head. Perceptual development often is driven by the value judgment that a parent or caregiver places on objects or subjects seen within the environment. The value judgment placed on the subject or object is further intensified by the emotionally assigned degree of intensity felt by the parent or caregiver. Assigned degrees of intensity are simply *levels of color-code biases* generated by our hearts or emotions and placed on animate and inanimate objects and also subjects encountered around the environment in which we live.

Family heads and caregivers in homes come in varied forms, and their roles are in diverse capacities; they may exist as biological parents, older siblings, surrogate parents (in foster homes), nannies, babysitters, and guardians. Children learn a lot from these adult figures through training and behavior modeling. The perceived fears, threats, and strength of these caregivers are modeled in real time and in behaviors and utterance likely to be picked up by the young, innocent child. In other words, the value judgment a caregiver places on others, coupled with the assigned degree of intensity to such a value, determines the kind of behavior and speech modeled in front of the young child, which, in turn, influences the child's acceptance or rejection of others.

For example, if an individual in social group A perceives someone in social group B as inferior or superior, the value judgment of inferiority or superiority assigned to the individual in social group B comes with an assigned degree of intensity, which may be either high (vivid) or low (dark). A high or vivid degree of intensity may indicate a less intense or slight hatred or mild dislike or even acceptance. Conversely, a low or dark degree of intensity is an indication of a profoundly strong hatred and dislike, or a deeply strong disapproval or absolute nonacceptance.

This same principle is applied in our daily lives when we view others at home, or pictures we see in museums or when we witness an incident involving another's action or inaction. That's why two or three different persons may be witnesses to the same incident in the same time frame, yet their accounts of what happened will have varying degrees of the truth, due to the assigned values of intensity placed on the objects or subjects involved in the incident. The narratives of each witness will be influenced by the perceptual value judgment placed on the individuals involved in the incident coupled with the assigned degree of value intensity (or color-code biases) given the value judgment placed on the individuals involved.

In other words, each witness's personal bias, based on knowledge stored as a result of training received, or previous ethnic, social, economic, or spiritual encounters, may tend to influence the value judgement placed, and the assigned degree of value intensity. Personal biases based on previous knowledge may determine the validity or truthfulness (or lack thereof) of the narrators' account of the incident. It is the same principle that determines, in most cases, the choosing of sides by an individual—whom to believe and whom not to believe.

Thus, the placement of value judgment and the assigning of degrees of value intensity are determined by the following:

- Training received by individual(s) in group A regarding the acceptance or rejection of individual(s) in group B
- Individual(s) in group A's previous encounter with the individual(s) in group B or someone who looks like them
- Individual(s) in group A's perceived insecurity or confidence in relation to the individual(s) in group B
- Individual(s) in group A simply dislikes the way the individual(s) in group B looks, talks, dresses, walks, or laughs or doesn't like the family, ethnic group, or race

Regardless of the cause, my assigned degree of intensity applied to the value judgment placed on individuals in group B will determine the strength of my rejection and hatred or my acceptance and love for individuals in group B. Amagnoh (2014) refers to this assessment as the "Chromatic Attribution System," while Dewey (1964) sees it as the "Aesthetic experience" or "conception of experience in its integrity." The same principle is what translates into any group's desire to dominate and rule others. Domination being a result of our assigned value-intensity constructs which feeds our ethnic, social, political, emotional, religious, economic, and spiritual ways of constructing or reconstructing value judgments of those who look and feel different from us.

VALUE SYSTEMS, AUTHORIZING ENVIRONMENTS, AND THE POINTILLIST PERCEPTION

Every home or family has a value system that is upheld and handed down from generation to generation. *Value systems* are age-long, operating traditions or norms held onto by institutions, or a social group, and have become bonded to the heart, mind, and soul of the group. Family-based value systems may cover the spiritual or religious, educational, economic, political, and social aspects of life in the home. It is the operating value system that feeds into the family environment and its atmospheres discussed in the previous section.

Value system considerations often require a scale of preference that ranks one concept of family life above another. In most instances, family heads are the ones who determine the scale of preference and values of utmost importance for the family. Once determined, the value that most likely grips the heart, mind, and soul of the family head becomes the single significant force that drives training, teaching, and instructions given to the young. The value of utmost importance is what controls and determines how the family head authorizes, grants, or denies access to social, political, economic, emotional, and spiritual or religious aspects of life in the family. Those values are then passed on through training and instruction, in order to keep the family's value system alive.

In addition, achieving continuity of family value systems requires both tangible and intangible structures—actions, or constructs—to be put in place or learned, with the tangible reinforcing the intangible. For the intangible structure, action, or construct to influence and take hold of the young child with the desired degree of intensity, it requires in most cases, the dishing out of tangible rewards or punishments to enforce adherence, or lack thereof, to the intangible. Tangible rewards or punishments may come in types and levels which signify the degree of intensity assigned the value placed on the intangible structure or action to be learned. In other words, the reward or punishment given must equate the level of importance or bias (degree of intensity in value) assigned the intangible structure, action, or construct the child has learned or has disobeyed. Consequently, the value placed on the intangible structure or construct determines the decisions, action or inactions of the authority figure—family head, or parent.

An *authorizing environment* therefore, is determined by the type and kind of headship controlling the environment's value system and the perceptual mindset that drives the actions or inactions of the head (Moore 1998)—how he or she gives commands, grants, denies, oversees, approves, or disapproves of (family) operations all determine the existing authorizing environment. Similarly, the family's activity or inactivity (pursuits or lack thereof) are managed and controlled by the authorizing environment. The management of the family's affairs is determined largely by the value judgment placed, and the degree of intensity assigned the value of a perceived threat or otherwise by the authorizing environment—the family-head.

I have mentioned earlier that an individual's or group's insecurities or security may result from a previous encounter that's often processed and stored as knowledge for future use. In some cases, such an individual's or group's value are assigned from afar without any justification, just as one would judge a book merely by its cover, instead of reading it before passing judgment. The 1988 romance comedy *Coming to America* vividly portrays how we, as individuals, place value judgment on others, whether they are close to us or afar. This ideal is not only morally wrong but also against the doctrine of building sound relationships for spiritual and social coexistence.

The *pointillist perception* or purview aims at placing individual families in a position of crafting values systems by which they approach each other with an open, nonjudgmental mindset. The pointillist purview advocates for family members to go through a process of exploration and discovery—a deliberate entry into the world of another (families) without any preconceived notions, ideas, or stereotypes. Entry into another's world may occur by getting together socially for fellowships, parties, movie nights, family dinners, games, picnics, conversations, and so on. Engaging in inter-family activities presents opportunities for individuals from different homes and backgrounds to get to know each other better and to understand and relate much more to their actions or inactions, as well as the circumstances of the other. Such activities help us to understand each other well, rather than instantaneous rejections based on looks, social standing, and so on. A pointillist perception of another allows the building of a social-relational value system based on an in-depth understanding of who we are, and what we do, and why and how we do and view things in a certain way, and act and deal with issues differently.

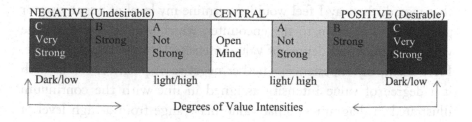

NEGATIVE (Undesirable)			CENTRAL		POSITIVE (Desirable)	
C Very Strong	B Strong	A Not Strong	Open Mind	A Not Strong	B Strong	C Very Strong
Dark/low		light/high		light/ high		Dark/low

Degrees of Value Intensities

Diagram 4. Value Development Continuum
with Degrees of Intensities
Source: Amagnoh (2014)

From a pointillist perspective, diagram 4, above, demonstrates what happens when I encounter another person in a secondary environment. First, central to the pointillist purview, it is in my interest and in the interest of the one I am meeting to approach the encounter with an open mind so that as the encounter unfolds through actions, inactions, narratives, and stories, I will be in a position, mentally and emotionally, to evaluate the experience. It is very important not to have preconceived notions of the other person before the encounter. Should that happen, there is a 100 percent chance it could cloud my ability to judge fairly. Depending on how I am received, listened to, attended to, comforted, or mocked, I may then be in a better position to make a decision, based on my experience during the encounter.

My encounter may be either desirable or undesirable, depending on how intensely I felt received or rejected during the encounter. I will now be able to assign and register mentally positive or negative degrees of value intensities, equivalent to what the continuum in diagram 4 illustrates. My experience may be given a particular value judgment and assigned a degree of intensity, ranging from a light or high, positivity desirability, to a dark, or low, negative desirability or rejection, and vice versa. Assigning a darker degree of intensity means I have a stronger negative opinion of the experience and the individual encountered. That said, the result of my experience could go either way, positive or negative, as illustrated in the diagram.

Similarly, actions and inactions during an encounter may result in an undesirable (or negative), desirable (or positive) experience. In that regard, the way I feel would determine my level of negativism or positivism in reaction to the encounter, which would determine the value judgment and degree of value intensity I assign the experience. Here again, my experience, whether negative or positive, brings with it a degree of value intensity assigned in line with the continuum illustrated in diagram 4. That value may range from a high level of negativity to a low level of negativity or otherwise. The darker or lower the assigned degree of intensity, the stronger the negative value assigned the experience encountered.

Also, the pointillist view of value creation can be explained by the phenomenon illustrated in diagram 5 below. In this illustration, the pictorial plain uses the juxtaposition of colored dots. Families across every society operate in a like manner, to colored dots placed side by side each other on a painter's canvas. Our societies, organizations, and institutions are just like a painter's canvas organized with colored dots of similar values and intensities. In a pointillist painting, colored dots with similar characters—in value and intensity—would gravitate toward each other to form larger pictorial plains as the viewer steps farther away from the canvas.

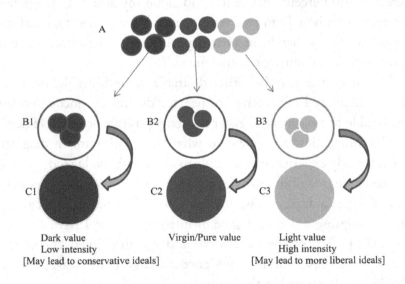

Diagram 5: Value Systems with Varied Intensities
Source: Amagnoh (2014)

For example, in diagram 5 above, we see a cluster of red dots, labeled A, placed closely against one another. That is how we find ourselves in our families and the larger society. We are just individual dots in the larger context of societal membership. When you come down to the next level of dots, labeled B1, B2, and B3, you begin to see the individual dots aggregating to form broader clusters of similar-color value intensities. Here in the diagram, cluster B2 is a virgin color—the pure, unadulterated form of the color red—while clusters B1 and B3 have value intensities different from cluster B2. The values of cluster B1 and B3 have changed to a darker and lighter value, respectively, because they have been mixed by another color. The introduction of another color causes cluster B2 to lose its originality to become B1 and B3.

Also, when you encounter another with an open mind, the experience encountered becomes a coloring on your perception of the other, resulting in a degree of value assigned that particular experience. Once you go farther down to the third level, labeled C1, C2, and C3, you will find that the cluster of dots is completely settled in and forms a solid picture of a different colored plain. So, color-plain C1, which previously was cluster B1, is now much more solid and maintains its dark value with a low degree of intensity, while color-plain C3, which was previously cluster B3, is also now much more solid and maintains its light value with a high degree of intensity.

This concept may explain why, in a large social gathering—school, college, or corporate settings—members of similar ethnicities, social standing, gender, or economic class tend to gravitate toward each other. The same principle might explain what happens when radical and nonradical individuals or groups begin to conscientize and indoctrinate new members. However, even within those larger groupings, there are still existing subgroups that gravitate toward each other based on their level of affluence and motivation levels within the larger group. The state of gravitation also depends on how dark or light the value of individual ideals of affluence and motivation is. A person with a positively dark, or low degree of value intensity may more likely lean toward conservative ideals, while the person with a positively light, or high degree of value intensity may more likely lean toward liberal ideals.

It therefore stands to reason that as a young child grows in the primary environment, the teachings, utterances, and practices, both overt and covert, will determine which value intensity is generated within his or her perceptive views. If he or she is treated with disdain and cruelty, talked to with no decency and respect for another, all what will be known to be his or her reality is cruelty and disdain for others. In effect, the negative, dark, and low level of value intensity stored as knowledge is what will be used to treat others in future secondary environments. Therefore, as parents and caregivers, we owe it to God and humanity to model for our children life lessons that are true to the will of God, for us, our children, and the larger society. Our actions and inactions must be based on the principles of truth, and love as outlined in the holy scriptures.

Furthermore, appreciating the circumstances of our children and others, through the pointillist prism of empathy and understanding is crucial. Listening to one another, sharing stories and narratives aid in the value judgments we place and assign in our hearts during the encounters we experience. Positive experiences lend us toward a more fruitful friendship, creating a deeper and meaningful social-relational experience in our hearts and minds, thereby impacting the knowledge we store for our future use. It provides an assigned degree of intensity that is of merit, regardless of what an individual looks like, how he or she talks, or what he or she eats or wears, or where he or she comes from.

It is crucial that, as parents, we always ensure that children interact freely and engage in conversations about themselves with others, be they siblings or peers, without prejudice. The values we parents teach and model must always be based on facts and not assumed fears or preconceived ideas. The pointillist ethos in itself, is a value system worthy of adoption and practice for every person, home or family, and society, as it does not allow rushed judgments about others. It advocates approaching an encounter and others with an open mind.

Christ teaches me to love the Lord my God, with all my heart, mind, and soul and to love my neighbor as myself— (Matt. 22:37 & 39). It is this fundamental social principle about building relationships and fellowships that we need to uphold in our families and communities. We always need to remind ourselves that it is solely because of the love

God the Father had for us which made Him give his only begotten Son as a sacrifice for our redemption and reconciliation unto Him. And it is love that compelled the Son to bear our sins, though He knew no sin. It is love that made Him accept a death reserved for only criminals. You and I therefore have an obligation, as parents and leaders in our families and as mentors of children, to ensure that love is always the driving force by which children see our actions and inactions. Love must be the social-lens through which we model behavior, as well as treat *any* child that comes our way.

SECTION 5
Relational Value:
Who (Uses It)?

Permit me to start this section with an encounter I had in the summer of 2002. It was my first summer since arriving in Ohio University in September 2001. Notwithstanding, I decided to take some summer courses in order to graduate ahead of schedule. At the end of classes one day, around midday, I decided to walk the thirty-minute trip home instead of going to the library, which was just a stone's throw away, to study. My idea was to go home, rest, and work on my assignments at night. The majority of students had gone on vacation, except those of us taking summer classes. Most departmental administrative staff were still working together with faculty, who were teaching classes that summer.

From the Geography Department, I slung my backpack on my left shoulder and walked past the Alden Library on to North Court Street, heading south. The usually busy North Court Street was almost desolate but for the few trucks and vans making deliveries to the restaurants and snack bars. I took a left turn onto West State Street, leaving downtown behind, and headed toward the 300 block, where my apartment was located. The farther I moved away from midtown, the quieter and more desolate the street became.

At one point, I crossed the street to use the pedestrian walkway on the other side. After getting on the walkway, I observed a chain of cars still parked along the street, which, I believed, belonged to students still on campus. I looked ahead and saw the first human since turning onto West State Street about seven minutes earlier. She was Caucasian, most likely a student, about one hundred feet ahead, and walking in my direction. I was gladdened, and I prepared mentally to greet her and possibly get to make another new friend.

Since arriving in OHIO in the fall, my objective had been to make as many acquaintances as possible, no matter their race or background. I had succeeded so far—until that moment. She was also carrying her backpack, presumably going to class or heading downtown for lunch or for some other transaction. My expectation was dashed against the rocks when, just about twenty-five feet away from making contact, she took a sharp right between two parked cars and walked into the middle of the street. She continued walking in the street as she passed me by and hardly turned to even look at me, let alone greet me.

I turned for one final glance, wondering what that was all about. To my surprise, I saw her walk on for about another ten steps and then take a sharp left between two other parked vehicles to get back to the walkway and continue her walk. *Oh, my goodness! She was actually avoiding me*, I thought. Why would she act like that? Was I that scary? What was she so afraid of? Why would she have a preconceived notion of me without even knowing who I am? My mind raced on with so many questions as I walked home.

Back in my apartment, I still ponded over what had transpired. I was actually disturbed and offended in a way. She had taken me for something or someone I was not. It hurt all the more, knowing that back in Ghana, I was always ready to assist foreign students who came to my part of the country for internships and research. I hosted some personally in my home and found surrogate parents for others when I didn't have enough room to host. Those students, to this day, regard me as family, a friend, and even a father, due to the care I gave them. But this experience was too much for me because of the mindset I had developed over the years toward fellow humans—that is, to be as open as I can be to all.

Finally, I decided not to let the incident bother me too much and to let it go. It would take a number of courses in African American Studies, and Multicultural Education in the United States to truly understand why that Caucasian student behaved in that manner. And in my opinion, it all came down to one word: *trust*.

Distrust of others can consume individuals, families, communities, and fellowships. It becomes mind-boggling when such distrust is so prevalent in a country known all over the world as the melting pot of all races and cultures. I am inclined to bring that experience into focus here because it speaks to obstacles in the way of building sound social relationships and, of course, relational value creation. That is why it is important, when it comes to relational value creation, to know what should be done—what it should take and the question of *who* should use it in the building of social relationships.

CRAFTING YOUR RELATIONAL VALUE

From a pointillist perspective, as established in the previous section, social relationships are built and relational value considerations achieved when, from the very start, there is open-mindedness on the part of individuals and social groups, when they are willing to engage themselves with cordiality. An open mind can only be the product of an open-heart that is willing to be receptive of another. As the saying goes, "It takes two to tango." A social engagement of such nature demands extra effort from both sides. Often, such social engagements start from a simple greeting—such as, "Good morning"—followed by the question, "How are you?" This simple but often difficult form of communication leads to amicable conversations, in most instances, and even getting to know each other with much deeper levels of dialogue.

One is reminded to think of the term *affection* in a friendship and *love* in a relationship. How affectionate a friendship may become between two people or the amount of love experienced in a relationship stems from the complete dictates and openness of an unflinching heart, by which the mind takes over with resolute fervor and passion. This type of love survives where most have failed, due to the fact that we take love many times as an investment, or is meant to show romantic intentions, and that's all. But to consider the true nature and form of love as God intends it to be within and among His people, it is more than just engaging in it for amorous reasons. It is more than engaging in it for exchange purposes or philanthropic reasons—the "I want something back in return for my love" kind of love. True love is God's love—the *agape* love, God's perfect and unconditional love. It is love shown and performed by God with nothing received in return; love given not based on merit; love that is sacrificial and wants nothing in return.

Similarly, love within the pointillist purview is considered as a performative acronym. It is a social theatrical staging, or an act experience, which demands the conscious presence of the heart and mind of the performer(s). This conscious presence of the heart and mind is needed during every scene until the love-act is completed. As a performative acronym, each letter that spells the word love—L-O-V-E—stands for a specific word or scene within the love-act; that is, *leave, overcome, venture,* and *empathize.* These four words, when well performed together, culminate into an overall social-relational love-act experience, strong enough to break down cultural, ethnic, racial, and/ or tribal barriers.

In my mind's eye, as a (social)pointillist, the *love-act* experience, as dramatized by the performer(s) comprises several unconcealed love scenes which together enhance the overall love-act. It is different from the act of love performances we experience in most friendships or relationships where the actual intent of the performer(s) is hidden until later.

In a *love-act* the performance, love is carried out regardless of whether there is a return value or not. The performer is less concerned about the return value but performs for the sake of aiding others. There is always that ideal assurance that drives the love shown, that is making life better for a fellow human without an expected outcome or regret. What Jesus did on the cross at calvary captures the essence of the love-act—the *agape* act. Also, the parable of the good Samaritan (Luke 10:25-37), told by Christ, epitomizes yet the substance of a true love-act heartily performed in the absence of a returned value and with no regrets.

On the other hand, an *act of love* is performed for as long as something is derived from love—returned value. A woman may perform an act of love onto a man simply because she derives a particular outcome(s) from the love performed—have a roof over her head, or get constant resources for a pedicure—and the same goes for a man too. An important personality in private or public service may have a male body guard who performs an act of love, ready to do anything for his boss, even place himself in the line of fire by taking a bullet for the boss. He performs such an act of love solely because of the return value he expects even if he dies. The valued return is the assurance that drives his love for the boss, solely for himself and his family. But, once the return value diminishes or is no longer there, the love performance also diminishes with little or no interest to resuscitate it.

Scripture talks about the endearing relationship God has with us: "But God demonstrates His own love towards us, in that while we were still sinners, Christ died for us" (Rom. 5:8). The book of John further speaks to this endearing relationship this way: "I am the vine, you are the branches. He who abides in Me, and I in him, bears much fruit; for without Me you can do nothing" (John 15:5). The apostle Paul reaffirms this position by way of cautioning us as believers, saying:

> Though I speak with the tongues of men and of angels, but have no love, I have become sounding brass or a clanging cymbal. And though I have the gift of prophecy, and understand all mysteries and all knowledge, and though I have all faith, so that I could remove mountains, but have not love, I am nothing. And though I bestow all my goods to feed the poor, and though I give my body to be burned, but have not love, it profits me nothing. Love suffers long and is kind; love does not envy; love does not parade itself, is not puffed up … And now abide faith, hope and love, these three; but the greatest of these is love. (1 Cor. 13:1–13)

The social-relational love-act experience, by virtue of the above texts, serves as the overarching principle or umbrella under which God's Son, Jesus Christ, performed among us and delivered His Ministry. That is, I believe, the reasons why Jesus asked: "Simon, son of Jonah, do you love Me more than these?" ... He said to him, "Feed my lambs." ... "Simon, son of Jonah, do you love Me?" ... He said to him, "Tend My sheep." He said to him the third time, "Simon, son of Jonah, do you love Me?" ... Jesus said to him, "Feed My sheep" (John 21:15-17). His questioning was with the understanding that Simon Peter is the rock upon which his Ministry will be established going forward. And any handling such responsibility needs to have an idea of His love-act performance or experience. It is by the same principle that God intends for us humans to deal with and treat each other.

With this understanding, the four words—leave, overcome, venture, and empathize—may be further understood as essential pillars of the love-act of Christ, revealed throughout His ministry and which must guide and support any meaningful relationship in our communities. Therefore, as parents, leaders, or socializing agents, we need to expand these four words (pillars) further, within the pointillist purview, into *social command statements* that will, inform our daily actions and inactions in our quest to build meaningful relationships, either within the family or in our neighborhoods. The following social command statements are demonstrable scenes, or performative statements which, when well executed, frame the overall love-act experience of any individual(s):

1. Leave your comfort zone.
2. Overcome your initial fears.
3. Venture into the unknown as a listener.
4. Empathize with understanding.

Individually and collectively, leave, overcome, venture, and empathy are words that help us to understand the kinds of efforts needed to encounter the world of another, and to fulfill the love-act performance or experience. Additionally, when accomplished, enables both parties to get firsthand insight into who the other person is and what he or she represents, believes, and stands for. Let's take the statements one by one and see how they play into the pointillist perception and ideal of building relationships or friendships.

Pillar 1: Leave Your Comfort Zone: To leave one's comfort zone or "step outside the box," as some would say, is the first scene in the act of discovery, encountering, building new and lasting relationships, and encountering new people, cultures, and ideas. Biblical accounts in the book of John indicate that the love of God propelled Him to give, "His only begotten Son, that whoever believes in Him should not perish but have everlasting life" (John 3:16). While this account is true, it is also true that it took an act of courage and compassion by the "only begotten Son" to leave His comfort zone—leave behind all the Father's wealth and riches, as well as the splendor of angels living at His beck and call—to come and serve humanity on earth. Jesus, had to step outside the box to be born a commoner by a simple handmaid, and in a manger—a feeding trough—and live the low life of a woodworker.

Jesus Christ experienced love in its ultimate from His Father, and He understands the love act, such that He was willing to come down wrapped in flesh and to serve under extreme challenges and circumstances; let alone be His Father's sacrificial Lamb so that, "We should be called children of God" (1 John 3:1). Often times we become comfortable in our ways, without making any attempt to step outside our regular routines and ways of life. We say, "I am the best," giving ourselves false notions of greatness as we wallow in our area of expertise. In many instances, we create false impressions of others, depending only on the narrative we have seen, experienced, or heard about.

My grandma once gave me a proverb in the Ewe language, which literally translates: "A child who has not traveled outside his or her hometown thinks the mother is the only one who prepares the tastiest soup." One day, by some design, that child visits another town and eats soup prepared by another woman and realizes that, all this while, he has been greatly mistaken—the mother's soup is not the tastiest. In fact, leaving our comfort zones gives an opportunity to test and compare other waters against the water with which we are already familiar. In that regard, I set myself up to experience that which had hitherto been unknown to me.

We read in the book of Genesis about Abram (whose name was later changed to Abraham) leaving his comfort zone upon the order of God: "Now the Lord had said to Abram: 'Get out of your country, from your family and from your father's house, to a land that I will show you'" (Gen. 12:1). For me to leave my kinsmen for a different agenda demands a 180-degree turn, away from the usual norms, traditions, ideals, values, culture, and philosophies that have, for ages, governed my life and the life of my kinsmen, whom I have grown to accept. It demands courage, since I will be harshly judged as the black sheep of the family. I will be mocked, scorned, despised by many, and labeled a deserter. I will be disowned and even suffer the loss of my inheritance.

On the other hand, we learn from this command and Abram's subsequent obedience to the command that leaving one's comfort zone in order to encounter a new experience is something that God wants for us, His children, because stepping out of my comfort zone will lead to God's move upon my life in ways unimaginable. I need to understand that there are some types of environments and atmospheres in which God cannot operate. Also, there are some types of people who, due to their spiritual inclination and attitudes, will not allow God to release blessings upon my life when I am constantly around them. God's will cannot manifest unless I separate myself from them or that particular environment. God always wants to set people apart for His blessings to manifest in their lives. Therefore, God had to instruct Abram to leave his kinsmen, his environment of comfort, and his pagan household in order to move in his life. Abram, with obedience, stepped out of his comfort zone, where he had lived all his life, and into the unknown. His only belief was obedience to a command he heard from a God he had never seen physically.

As a social being, a believer, and follower of Christ, I do not have to know somebody in order to help out, or encounter his or her world. For all I know, the encounter is God-purposed—an encounter meant to grant the miracle I have been waiting for, or an opportunity to be of help and a blessing to the person encountered. Christ underscores this fact through the parable of the Good Samaritan, presented in Luke 10:25–37, when a certain lawyer asked Jesus, "And who is my neighbor?" (Luke 10:29). We need to remember that the importance of approaching and helping others in need or in trouble—no matter who they are or where they come from—is paramount to our very survival in many ways. In Exodus 2:16–17, scripture reveals the heart and attitude of Moses toward the seven daughters of Reuel, the priest of Midian—how he rescued the seven girls from rough, inconsiderate male sheepherders and helped draw water for them to water their flocks. All it takes is trust, courage, perseverance, and the right attitude.

Abram trusted the God who spoke to him. He mastered courage to take a chance and leave his comfort zone on the word of an unseen God. Without knowing the outcome, he persevered to accomplish the command given him. And all he took along was his trust in an unseen deity and his positive attitude. Many have lost great chances and blessings in life, simply because they failed to trust themselves, let alone, somebody. They never gathered courage to try anything new or approach any other who didn't look like them, or speak like them to experience something different. They failed to persevere by giving up too easily in the midst of the slightest adversity, and their attitude is always to demean others. Like Nathanael, they came to rapid conclusions about others, saying, "Can anything good come out of Nazareth?" (John 1:46).

There is another side to leaving one's comfort zone, and that is trying to engage in the language, culture, dance, music, arts, foods, and all socially engaging activities of the other person, who may not be a member of our cultural group. Even when we are from the same cultural group, there are still different ways in which clans, families, and/or households tackle issues or engage in the production or reproduction of their cultural artifacts. It is very important for us to step out of our feel-good environments and engage others around us, no matter how frivolous their ideas or personalities may seem.

Engaging in the culture of others does not mean I am abandoning my group's way of doing things or the Christian values I've upheld over the years. No, not at all. In John 17:14–15, before Jesus's departure to His Father, He understood that just as the world hated Him, they would do the same to His disciples and followers because He made the Word—the truth—know to us. Christ went further to ask His Father not to take us, His followers, out of the world but to protect us from the evil one. He was aware beyond every doubt that for His Father to take

His followers out of the world would mean His Word too would leave with them. Should that happen, His teachings and ultimate sacrifice would be in vain, since the world would be left without the Word. He expressed to His Father that His followers were not of this world, just as He was not, and He asked that the Father might sanctify His followers by the truth, since His Word, which He had given them (us) is truth.

Engaging the world of the other grants me the opportunity to introduce and establish in his or her life the truth about God's Word. Having said that, it is our duty to be equipped with the principles of that truth and be focused on those things that will edify and uphold the truth in us, no matter how occupied we are. We must try to understand and accommodate others, whether they are believers of the faith or unbelievers—rejoice with them when they are rejoicing, mourn with them when they are mourning—but be as wise as the serpent to not be lured into the trappings of their environment. When an unbelieving family is celebrating the success of any member, you and I, followers of Christ, can join in celebrating with them and be happy for them. But I also must understand that their unbelief is assigned from my Christian value perspective. Surely that family also has something they believe in, only their belief system does not align with mine.

Therefore, I have to show strength and not succumb to the trappings that exist in their alternate environment. Such trappings may include activities like drinking of alcoholic beverages, speaking profanity and curse words, hatred for others, and so on. No matter how long it takes, our ability to exist and interact with sincerity in an environment of unbelief will ultimately draw them into our world of faith in Christ Jesus. It is how we carry ourselves—with circumspection and love, with open hearts and minds as we join them in celebrations—that is a key to winning trust.

I remember when I became born again. I had a surprise visit from three brothers with whom I used to imbibe alcoholic drinks. They took me out, with my wife's permission, to a liquor bar. They ordered a case of lager beer and a bottle of dry gin, declaring that it was our evening of celebration, since they hadn't seen me in years. That evening, I rejoiced and celebrated the reunion with them, but all I requested throughout the evening was bottles of Coca-Cola drink. I was reminded by scripture:

"Therefore, if anyone is in Christ, he is a new creation; old things have passed away; behold, all things have become new" (2 Cor. 5:17). I knew who I used to be and who I had become and that I should hold up myself before others by adhering to Christian principles that set the believer apart from the world.

In fact, those brothers were truly amazed that day, considering the amount of alcohol we used to quaff together. Even though they teased me throughout the evening and told me I was building a "museum of worms" in my stomach, due to the sugar I was dumping there, I could see in their eyes and read from their words and demeanor that they were fully aware that something had actually happened—something had changed in me that they needed to know. That recognition alone was sufficient, and most important, they did realize that if I had changed, then they too could change.

Pillar 2: Overcome Your Initial Fears: Once you decide to leave your comfort zone and you succeed in doing so, the next demonstrable scene is the task of overcoming the initial fear that grips you and prevents you from engaging in a conversation. Yes, we often decide to step out, but we freeze in the attempt to make the next move by speaking to the other person with a simple greeting. The *spirit of fear* is a dangerous and self-limiting spirit. It overtakes and cripples our most-desired ability of self-belief. It comes from a very deep and dark side of the heart, challenging the Spirit of God in us—the very essence of God that teaches us to recognize and understand our potentials as children of God.

Even if I have not yet accepted Christ as my personal Savior, the breath of God is still in me and must give me cause to live a fearless and fulfilled life among others. I need to remember always that Satan, the angel and master of darkness, plants the spirit of fear in my heart, using it as a self-limiting and clever weapon of distrust and misgiving, in order for me to doubt my potential and existence as a child of the Most High God. Do not ever doubt because you are a child of God, the Lord of light. And from the position of a child of light, your confidence must be firmly planted in scripture from the book of Philippians, which says, "I can do all things through Christ who strengthens me" (Phil. 4:13). Therefore, whenever you feel threatened by your inner emotions or you feel discouraged about approaching and speaking with a stranger or someone you have seen before but never spoke to, don't underestimate your potential as a child of the Most High. Approach with confidence and speak out, knowing and believing, "You are of God ... and have overcome them, because He who is in you is greater than he who is in the world" (1 John 4:4).

As a child of the God, fear must not be part of your vocabulary because in the kingdom of God—and, for that matter, the kingdom of light—fear is *not* given any value. And I can say with absolute certainty that the spirit of fear is nonexistent in God's kingdom. You cannot find the spirit of fear in the presence of light. The word *fear* does not exist in angelic vocabulary or in the emotional conduct of God, and for that matter, all heavenly beings. It is the nonexistent nature and presence of fear in heaven that gives heaven's angelic messengers cause to address humans, first and foremost, with reassurance and with the phrase, "Fear not."

Introducing the spirit of fear into the emotions of humankind was and still remains the strategic weapon used by Satan against the followers of Christ and members of the kingdom of light here on earth. Fear is the main tactical weapon used to usurp and rob you and me of the spirit of boldness, self-belief, and trust in the Holy Spirit—the Spirit who comes to resides in our hearts once we accept Christ as our Lord and Savior. Once saved, the devil and his cohorts will always attempt to use fear as a weapon to generate pessimism, unbelief, doom and gloom, and self-doubt in your heart, as a believer and follower of Christ. Therefore, you must be bold, and overcome your initial fears by trusting the Holy Spirit to grant you the enablement.

The apostle Paul, in his second letter to Timothy, makes this enablement very clear and reassuring: "For God has not given us a spirit of fear, but of power, and of love and of a sound mind" (2 Tim. 1:7). The Holy Spirit does not have a timid personality, neither is He afraid to take up challenges of any sort. On the contrary, the Holy Spirit exudes limitless power, boldness, kindness, and love, with an immeasurably dose of self-discipline. Therefore, whoever has the Holy Spirit must also, without reservation, exhibit the same qualities, unless that person does not believe. But the good news is, Christ has given us the opportunity to claim that power and boldness of the Holy Spirit by the simple act of confessing Him as our Lord and Savior and being baptized by immersion in water to become born again as a child of God. This simple act gives us power to do all things through Christ Jesus, who gives the believer strength.

Unfortunately, as believing families, many of our homes, marriages and relationships experience the spirit of fear, manifesting under a different label, yet similar in its fundamental emotions. It is the *spirit of jealousy*. Like fear, jealousy comes from a deeply imagined state of insecurity, in which the individual who is jealous sees the subject of jealousy as a possession, rather than a God-sent helper. I am of the opinion that taken as a possession, the subject of jealousy can easily be thrown away, just as I would discard an object like a wristwatch or a hat that I previously guarded passionately and prevented its use by another. However, the hat or wristwatch soon becomes unappealing to me and becomes easily disposable, once I lose interest, or the object possessed becomes old. Let me caution here: Your partnership, relationship, or friendship in social life is not a possessive enterprise; rather, it is an enterprise with the fundamental purpose of helping and complementing each other to overcome adversity, while also rejoicing together in successes achieved. This ideal is very important, particularly when it comes to the institution of marriage and family life.

That said, let me say with conviction that in every home, jealousy may emerge as a product of fear, if care is not taken. There are three distinct types of jealousy that may rattle a marriage or a relationship. And it is even possible for a relationship to encounter more than one of the three jealous positions, if not all, in the home or within the same relationship. They include:

- Jealousy of past partners
- Jealousy of not being first on the scene
- Jealousy of subsequent competitors

Jealousy of past partners: There are instances when spouses or friends get into petty arguments and quarrels, simply because they saw or heard that their significant other still chats with an ex. This sense of insecurity originates from the deep fear that my man or my woman may still be in love with an ex-spouse, or ex-boyfriend/girlfriend whom, by the way, I have succeeded in replacing. This jealous state becomes much more dangerous when my mind is constantly reminding me that I am not his or her first, and those I succeeded in displacing may still be lying in wait behind the scenes, aiming for a comeback at the least chance.

Jealousy of not being first to be on the scene: This kind of jealousy is grounded in the knowledge of how good, serviceable, romantic and wonderful my spouse, boyfriend, or girlfriend is—funny, kind, serviceable, beautiful, handsome, tantalizing, and flirty. These qualities in my partner gives me a satisfying emotional feeling, yet I have a dreaded sense of not being the first to unwrap and experience such remarkable displays of heightened sensual affection and passion. My fear may even become greater when I hold on to the idea that those who have encountered my significant other before I met him or her may someday want to come back, should they fail to get someone comparable to him or her out there. This kind of jealousy is the result of the frightful knowledge of not being the first to experience and enjoy such affectionate qualities I admire so much in my companion. It is a position of mind that could also lead to instances where I am gripped with fear any time my significant other gives attention to another man or woman, whether at church, parties, or any other social gathering.

Jealousy of subsequent competitors: This is a kind of jealousy which is not only exhibited by some spouses in their marriages, but is also revealed in boy-girl relationships and even in young children. It happens when the man or woman or a child has a heightened fear of losing his or her present love and affection to another or one presumed to be a rival or competitor.

I must admit I have been a victim of this kind of jealousy many years ago in a boy-girl relationship. Permit me to briefly recount what happened: I was then in secondary school, in my second year of a five-year program—the equivalence of high school in the U.S.—when I met Genevieve (pseudo name used for confidentiality), and we fell in love. We were natives of the same township, but while I was attending an all-boys Catholic boarding school which was about sixteen miles away from home, she had just entered her first year in a coeducation boarding institute, 50 miles away from my school. We used to exchange handwritten letters expressing our love and affection for each other: "I will cross the trackless deserts, swim the deepest oceans, and climb the highest mountains just to reach your love, my love," were some of the cajoling words I recall using in one of my letters to her. They were the days before electronic mails, and it was always a joy to read her responses neatly written in cursive. I would read her letters over and over after preps, and place them under my pillow while asleep, with the hope of having romantic dreams about the love we had for each other.

I had just returned to school in my third year, after an awful compound fracture I suffered during a football match, which kept me away from school for almost three months, when I received a letter from her. It was in response to the latest I had written her. She was now in her second year, but the tone in this letter was different from all I had previously received from her. She accused me of using words in my letter which she didn't like. In fact, I was taken aback. That night, I did a lot of mental gymnastics, trying to recollect what exactly I had written in my last letter which could have triggered such a response. There were no cell phones or telephones to communicate with instantly, neither was there a number I could dial even if I had a telephone available, so I had to wait till the holidays.

By this time, she stopped responding to my subsequent letters of inquiry. My situation was even worsened by the fact that my financial resources, were inadequate to embark on the 50-mile trip to see her. Hmm! I loved Genevieve and I couldn't afford to lose her. Even though I have resolved crossing the trackless deserts just to reach her love, I couldn't do so when it mattered most. All I could do was wait until holidays. The holidays did come and I visited her in the house, but she gave me cold shoulders. She wouldn't see me, neither would she read notes I sent to her through my little sister. The notes came back with the carrier, intensifying my heartache and agony.

My mother was aware of our relationship since I had introduced Genevieve to her right from the beginning. She would visit us often at home and mom treated her just like her own daughter. We were about three weeks into the holidays and mom was beginning to suspect that something wasn't right. She asked me why her visits had become very spasmodic. I had no choice, but to tell mom what was going on. She then decided to call Genevieve and get to the bottom of the matter, since she also noticed the situation was weighing me down and I had lost appetite, for she knew how excellent I was in doing justice to my meals.

So, mom invite her over and pressured her to say what exactly I had done or said which hurt her feelings. After many attempts, she finally told my mom it wasn't me, but rather, a senior girl at school: "My best friend ("Suppies" we call them at school) who read a letter George wrote me in my absence, and told me to respond to him in an angry manner," she said. She went on: "The senior girl wanted me to break up with George in order to start a new relationship with a senior boy in the school. She said the boy would make a better-fit for me than my so-called George. I had no choice but to comply with her proposal." Genevieve was in tears at that point.

My mother made me sit in during the interrogation, and after hearing all that Genevieve had said, I felt let down, and a jealous rage arose inside me: "So you decided to through all that we had away just to satisfy some senior girl's whims and caprices?" I asked, with no response from her. "Well, I guess that boy was your preferred choice that is why you easily gave in without a fight, so I wish you, your boyfriend, and your crocodile-tears well," I continued, as I stood up instantly to leave the meeting. Mom told me to take my time to resolve the issue, but I didn't listen to her and I stormed out of the meeting.

My little sister walked Genevieve home that evening after the meeting. My anger and ego took the better part of me and I couldn't see the situation from Genevieve's perspective. I refused to accept her incessant apologies. The days following saw her visit me almost every day, but I would go out to the movies immediately she entered our house. I would return late at night to find my pillow soaked in her tears. After a week, she had dropped about 60 pounds in weight and grew very skinny by the time we were heading back to school after the holidays. I stopped writing her throughout the rest of my secondary school days and went on to college.

We later got back on speaking terms, but I couldn't bring myself to continue the boy-girl relationship that existed between us. We all went our separate paths, after secondary school, I went on to study agricultural science education at a teacher training college, and I heard later, she had also gone to study agricultural extension in one of the agricultural colleges. She later left for further studies in Europe, while I pursued my career as a classroom teacher. Our paths crossed again once after about 12 years and we spoke for about an hour. I never saw her again until I heard of her tragic death in a car accident 21 years ago.

Up until her untimely death, I was told, Genevieve never got married nor bore any children. When I heard of her demise, and going down memory-lane, recounting all that transpired between us, I realized she did actually love me, and decided not to go in for any other after the break-up. I knew then I had acted selfishly, but again I was young, naïve, and immature in the handling of the entire situation. What's more, I never listened to my mother, who begged me to give her a second chance. I was afraid of a subsequent competitor, and driven by jealous emotions, I act in a very immature manner. Such is the impact of a jealous heart and mind on relationships when care is not taken.

When I became born again 20 years ago, I ask God for forgiveness for the decisions I took and the pain I caused Genevieve. The fact is, if God can forgive us our sins no matter how grievous they are, if He is a God of second chances, then who are we not to forgive our fellow humans when they offend us. By my Jealous emotions, I considered Genevieve as a personal possession, which I easily discarded, rather than seeing her as a gift God had brought into my life and as a friend and nothing else. Till this day, I always tell myself: "If I could turn back the clock of time I would have acted differently." But, in all, I am convinced God has forgiven me, and I would only make sure not to repeat such a mistake. All it takes is a little bit of patience, and the composure not to act on impulse but rather, to self-reflect before taking an important decision.

In some cases, a husband may become jealous when a baby is born, and the wife's attention shifts to the newborn, especially when the baby is a boy. Suddenly, a whole new world is created in the wife's life that occupies and draws her attention from the husband onto the new addition to the family. At this point the husband assumes that the usual attention the wife gives him has diminished due to the arrival of the newborn child. This notion of losing a wife's attention in marriage due to the birth a child can be equally dangerous to the very survival of the marriage. In extreme instances, some men, fearing they'll lose their wife's love and attention to a newborn, may decide not to have children at all in the marriage.

Similarly, a first child who has enjoyed considerable affection and love from the mother may reject a newborn in the family, due to the fear of losing his or her mother's love and affection. The rejection may even become worse when he or she notices that the mother's attention has shifted to the newborn overnight. That fear and state of mind presupposes that the mother's love will not come back because of to the newborn baby. The resultant fear leads to jealous emotions, which may lead to aggressive behavior toward the newborn brother or sister. Or it may lead to sulking in order to receive the mother's attention.

All these fears result from dark thoughts that seek to erode trust and self-confidence in a spouse, a family member, friend, and even parents. We always need to be guided by scripture, remembering that when we received Christ and were baptized in water, and we received the Holy Spirit, we became new creations in Christ Jesus, as expressed earlier, through 2 Corinthians 5:17. Therefore, as children of the Most High God, the fear of the unknown and jealous emotions must not be our portion in life nor in His kingdom here on earth.

I know people or believers who try to defend their jealous tendencies by saying, "Even God is a jealous God, so I can also be jealous of what I have." Yes, it is true, our God is a jealous God. He is jealous because He has every right to guard what He has created—you and me. He formed man out of dust in His own likeness and breathed into him the breath of life, and man become a living soul. And God loves man, His creation. We are His possessions because He created us. You and I should ask ourselves whether we've ever created any human being. We cannot even create a strand of hair on our heads, let alone form a living soul. You did not create the child you gave birth to. God formed that child in the woman's womb. Until you and I reach the point of creating our own spouses, children, boyfriends, and girlfriends, we have no right to be jealous over them when they come into our lives as loving gifts from God.

The fear of the unknown and the accompanying sense of insecurity that grips the heart can result in very undesirable actions or inactions. Such fears may even have dangerous consequences when acted out. For instance, what starts as the fear of subsequent competitors or the fear of past partners might lead me to jealousy; that jealous emotion then leads me to anger; and my anger could turn me into exhibiting aggressive behavior towards my spouse or friend, when care is not taken. My aggressive action or behavior could ultimately result in murder and a violation of one of God's Ten Commandments: "You shall not murder" (Ex. 20:13). So, you see what fear can cause us to do, if we do not eliminate it from our hearts completely, or exercise maximum constraints towards one another when it comes to building our relationships.

To eliminate fear in our relationships takes trust, and assistance from the power of the Holy Spirit, who resides in our hearts and empowers us to do the right thing. I am reminded of a poem I learnt many years ago, in kindergarten; it literally translates from the Ewe language like this: "There is a small bell in my heart; it sounds so loud when it rings. Anytime I do good, it gives me joy and happiness. But, when I do something bad, it worries me night and day." Yes, that small bell is, in fact, the Holy Spirit—what others may interpret as conscience. He exists in a child's heart right from conception, and we parent and leaders have a duty to foster Him, so that He might establish a stronghold on the conscience of the young child before becoming a young adult.

As a believer, you must rest assured that you and your family's situation is different from any other's. The plan of our God is never the same for everybody. As no two persons' thumbprints are the same, nor are the writings in the palms of our hands, so are the plans of God. To each and every one of us is assigned a specific divine will, according to God's timing and purpose, and revealed individually. Therefore, all you and I need to do is to trust Him, knowing that He is our Father and will not allow anything to happen to us.

Remember, you are God's child, and as individual 1, you are different from individual 2, when it comes to God's will and timing for your life. Your challenges, circumstances, and opportunities are different from any other person's. It doesn't matter if we were born single, twins, triplets, or what have you. We are all under different divine wills and plans, according to His purpose through Christ Jesus. Therefore, do not fear when individual 2 seems to be an adversary to your marriage or friendship, or is doing well in life than you are. Your conditions, circumstances, and challenges are not the same, despite the fact that you may be experiencing the same climate. Even then, your ability to absorb the heat or cold is still not the same as someone else's. Let this be your guiding principle in life and in facing life's challenges and adversities. I have grown over these years to understand and believe that, fear is the devil's weapon and trick, to distract me from the divine will and purpose of the living God for my life, and so must you.

Pillar 3: Venture into the Unknown as a Listener: You have managed to leave your comfort zone and have overcome your initial fears. It is now time to perform the next scene—to venture into the unknown world of the other, and as a listener.

It starts with a simple, "Hello, how are you?". Sometimes it is difficult to initiate such a first move, but when you try it, the result, in most cases, is amazing. We have reached a point in our lives where it is not easy to initiate a one-on-one dialogue with a neighbor or interact with one another. Twenty-first-century technologies and social media platforms have made it even more difficult to engage one another face-to-face. What's more, the surge of the global pandemic in 2020, with the resultant skepticism about a neighbor's healthiness, accompanied by the need for social distancing, and the lockdowns and face masks, have all made an already grim social-relational condition even worse. Nevertheless, we need to understand that a simple hello sets the stage for a one-on-one interaction, once we put our minds to it.

I felt extremely out of place, particularly when it came to daily interactions when I first entered the United States and started school in OHIO. Everyone on campus seemed so busy and had no time to stop for a moment and exchange greetings. My first impression was that on American streets, warm brotherly and sisterly interactions were rare occurrences, replaced often, in passing, with what art historians refer to as the "archaic smile" or what I suppose Frank McCourt refers to in his book *Angela's Ashes* as a "sneaky little Presbyterian smile" (1997). That so-called sneaky presbyterian smile in most cases is neither a smile nor grin; the facial expression occurred vaguely and half-heartedly within a very minimal time frame, after which the face immediately returned to its original stone-cold serious mood.

I always wondered about this kind of pace, and it troubled me because in Africa, we have time for each other—time to greet each other when we met on the streets and to inquire about each other's health and well-being during those moments of interaction. Such greetings even explore the well-being of parents, spouses, children, and entire families, not to mention the welfare of livestock as well. It gave me the feeling that someone does care about me as a person. Some may interpret or characterize this customary way of life as prying too much into another's private life, yet I have grown to believe it is the most satisfying, fulfilling, and graciously humane social interactivity that I could ever hope for in life. Besides, in Africa, it stands to reason that since it takes a village to raise a child, one needs to know how everyone and everything in that big village family is doing. A simple, genuine hello, coupled with an exploratory question— "How are you?"—is good enough to make someone's day or start a lifelong relationship. Taking the initiative to ask how another is doing, stranger or not, is essential in the creation and building of social relations.

Another important aspect of taking the initiative is for me to be ready to spare my time. Sparing some time to give others our attention and a listening ear could be the greatest gift we would ever give a stranger, who might be hurting and might need someone to listen to his or her story. You may be surprised to know how much it means to someone who just needs an ear to pour his or her challenges into. Through the act of giving a listening ear to a friend or a total stranger, you may open up a new pathway into a relationship or friendship that previously was unknown. Through interaction and words of encouragement, I may learn later that what I did—that little time we spared—turned out to be a blessing to the receiver or even myself. It is most fulfilling when you later realize or learn that through your gift of a listening ear, you stopped someone from causing self-harm. There also have been times when individuals have encountered God's angelic beings and have been blessed by sparing the time to engage a stranger who needed a listening ear.

Pillar 4: Empathize with Understanding: The fourth and final scene in the love-act is demonstrating empathy with understanding. The words *empathy* and *understanding* may seem similar, but they are not. Understanding is considered a mental process of recognition, conceptualizing or comprehension, or a state in which the mind comes to grips with an issue, while empathy is the knowledgeable recognition of the thoughts, feelings, and the overall state of a person. Also, empathy is the ability to emotionally place myself in another person's position or perspective. It comes with a sense of shared sentiments or feelings, while trying to identify with or understand why the person is feeling that way.

Commenting on empathy, Maya Angelou once said, "I think we all have empathy. We may not have enough courage to display it" (Angelou quotes 2020). Maya Angelou might have been liberal in a sense, by implying that all persons have some amount of empathy. I am tempted to differ from her position because it's not that some can't master enough courage, but they are just stone-cold in their reaction to the feelings and emotions of others. It does not come from the lack of courage, but the way they have been raised in their environment of growth. While understanding requires a mental action of absorbing and assimilating, without any possible emotional underpinnings, empathy engages the thoughts and emotions of the listener to the point where he or she feels the pain or joy expressed through the story in the narrative. It is the reason why the biblical drama, *The Passion of the Christ* (Gibson 2004) captured the attention of most viewers and drew many to tears while watching the movie.

One may safely conclude that while understanding may demand only the use of the mind or intellect, empathy uses the mind and adds the intrinsic motivations of the heart, which puts the person listening or seeing the drama unfold right in the shoes of the narrator or victim. Former president Barack Obama once voiced his opinion on the subject of empathy: "The biggest deficit that we have in our society and in the world right now is an empathy deficit. We are in great need of people being able to stand in somebody else's shoes and see the world through their eyes" (Obama quotes 2021). Empathy comes much more readily when you've been in the same or similar situation as the narrator or victim, when you know full well how it feels like to be in such a circumstance. That is not to say that empathy is the preserve of only those who have gone through similar experience or encountered similar life challenges. Not at all. It just takes a shorter time for such persons to identify with the circumstance and for it to register much more vividly with them, as opposed to someone who has no prior experience with the situation in question.

Since her days in second grade, my ten-year-old daughter has exhibited immense fear anytime there is a tornado warning, or a weather forecast with an imminent rainstorm, or when there is a rainstorm accompanied by intense thunder and lightning. She cries uncontrollably and clings to her mother while burying her face deep into her clothes. This fear of rainstorms has gone on in spite of our efforts to reassure her that she is safe because we are all together and nothing will happen to her.

Our encouragements notwithstanding, she didn't seem to get over her fear for storms—until recently when we understood why. On Monday, September 7, 2020, the tornado sirens went off at about 4:30 p.m. Radio and television broadcasts announced an imminent tornado, with wind gusts of about forty miles per hour hitting central Ohio. As we were preparing to have dinner, our city was mentioned on the radio as being among those in the path of the tornado. My daughter was so afraid, she rejected all appeals to eat her dinner. The entire family tried to console her and alleviate her fears with words of encouragement— that everything was going to be okay; that God was not going to allow anything to happen to us or her; that through His promises, He would never leave us nor forsake us. But she continued to cry uncontrollably. At this point, we were worried that this fear of storms had been going on for too long and, if not remedied, it could be a challenge for her in her adult life. My wife then decided to dig a little deeper into why she always was so afraid, since she hadn't been as a little girl. Besides, our family had never been in a critical storm situation, so where is this fear coming from, we wondered. She then decided to tell her when it all began and why she was fearful of storms that are accompanied by thunder and lightning.

She said, "When I was in the second grade, my teacher showed us a video in class on tornadoes and storms and the effects they have on people who those storms affected—their homes and livelihood. I saw in that video how people suffer after tornadoes and rainstorms hit their homes, stores, and farms and how they suffer in order to put their lives back. So, when there is a rainstorm or tornado warnings like today, I am so afraid for the people who will be affected. That is why I am so afraid." For a few moments, we were all silent. Her big sister was the first to break the silence. "Wow! That's empathy right there," she said. "Wow!" exclaimed the rest of us after her sister's initial comment. Yes, you may not have to be a victim of a terrible situation in order to empathize with others who are going through it. The intrinsic capability to have compassion is a virtue which we all need to strive for, no matter our social standing in life.

Her mother and big sister took turn to counsel her on what to do under such circumstances in order to overcome her fear. They advised her to start thinking about little projects she could put together in order to assist those affected by such disasters. Such an act they said, would give her fulfilment, as well as bring her comfort in knowing that the affected persons are being taken care of. They told her it was a good thing to empathize with others in their circumstances, but it would be even better if she thought about ways that she could assist those who are dislocated from their homes through such disasters. And it didn't matter whether she was young or old; she always could think of ways in which to help others in need. It was a very revealing moment for us all because we had assumed that she was acting up for no reason. It was truly our learning moment.

My observation over the years suggests to me that a parent, child, or a leader who is born into wealth and has never lacked food, shelter, and clothing will not appreciate another's story of lack—going to bed without a meal; having to brace against the cold and rain on the streets or in windowless, uncompleted structures; having to walk barefoot or wear one dress until it is threadbare and turning to rags. These life experiences cannot readily be understood by a leader, child, or parent born into riches, though they may somehow learn to appreciate such misfortunes along the way.

It is important to encourage ourselves, as parents, caretakers, leaders, and educators of children, to model empathy as we encounter stories from others who do not look like us, smell like us, speak or dress like us. Empathizing does not mean pitying the subject; it does not mean setting up the victim as a subject of ridicule. It demands that we all apply genuine concern and emotional understanding for all real-life situations that affect others. When possible, always empathize by trying to find ways to solve the problem in question, rather than making it a subject of ridicule or gossip to members of our kind. Showing genuine concern could be by way of giving words of assurance, encouragement, and comfort, and providing some form of (physical) assistance in addition to our heartfelt compassion.

WHO QUALIFIES TO USE RELATIONAL VALUE?

Every profession requires undertaking some form of training and education in the intended career of choice over a period of time. Once I have trained to pursue a particular career path, I cannot change paths without the needed education and training in that new area of choice. It will be impossible for me to perform well and excel in the new profession of choice. For instance, I cannot train as a lawyer and then decide along the way to be a medical doctor with the training acquired in law, and vice versa. You may try your hardest to succeed in the job you never had any form of training for, but it wouldn't be long before word would circulate about your performance and lack of credentials. You would be considered a fraud. In fact, for you to succeed in that new job without training would take a good measure of God's grace.

I mentioned earlier that all human beings are born equal, but the environment sets the stage for differences in character and behavior. Because we are all born equal and to human parents to whom we relate naturally as social beings, we already have the instinct in us to love and be relatable to others, and others to us. But the problem arises when our parents, in the primary environment, teach and train us in ways that may push people away from us or pull us away from others. This *push-pull factor* also may come into play as we move away from our primary environment to engage objects and subjects within a secondary environment. The point is, our parents may train us in the best possible ways to be relatable to others, but the kind of secondary environment we find ourselves in can interfere with our early training and education. The ability to withstand family pressures and other forms of pressure from the secondary environment is ours to navigate as we continue to grow.

It stands to reason that when asking who qualifies to use relational value, it is the person capable of creating and developing a relational ethos or attitude—in an environment governed with the embodiment of love and by the practice of the four command statements that I have discussed in this section.

I have to leave my comfort zone first. Without leaving my comfort zone, I cannot achieve the rest of what it takes to relate with others. Then, I have to overcome any fears of rejection or inferiority complexes that may serve as a hindrance to my ability to communicate with them. I have to also venture into the world of others by granting them my listening ear during the period of dialogue and interactivity. Then, of course, I need to empathize with others in need, and with understanding, placing myself in their shoes as a cementing force in order to bond with them and their world. When possible, I must try my best to find little but meaningful solutions to their situation. Without early training through behavior modeling and practice by my parents, in the four command areas, chances are learning and practicing the true love-act of Christ will be nonexistent in me. It will take God's grace to exhibit such acts in my secondary environments.

In the book of Matthew chapter 19, we read about a young man who asked Jesus: "Good teacher, what good thing shall I do that I may have eternal life?" (Matt. 19:16). Jesus answered him: "But if you want to enter into life, keep the commandments" (Matt. 19:17b). He responded: "Which ones?" (Matt. 19:18a). Jesus then gave him a reminder of the ten commandments, to which he responded: "All these I have kept from my youth. What do I still lack?" (Matt. 19:20). And Christ said to him, "If you want to be perfect, go, sell what you have and give to the poor, and you will have treasure in heaven; and come, follow Me" (Matt. 19:21).

And the bible says, "But when the young man heard that saying, he went away sorrowful, for he had great possessions" (Matt.19:22).

The young man could not bring himself to selling his riches to give to the poor, simply because as a young child, such an act has never been modeled for him to see and practice. I believe he was always reminded as a young child to guard his family's riches with his life. So, the idea of selling them to give to the poor pushed him away from Christ, his secondary environmental encounter. The young man's heart, mind and soul resides with his earthly riches and the prestige it generates in society. He could not comprehend why he should sell (and lose) all that to some ideal of building heavenly treasures. Not only that, abandoning his wealth just to follow Christ was to him unimaginable.

The bible teaches me in relation to this young man's encounter with Christ that where my treasure is, there shall my heart be also. What it also tells me is that any love-act, I perform towards others, by way of giving, is a crucial component to my personal salvation, earthly blessings, and true fellowship with God aside that I am imitating what the restorative love-act of Christ has done for me. The crucial nature of the love-act is the reason why the apostle Paul gives the reminder: "Therefore, my beloved, as you have always obeyed, not as in my presence only, but now much more in my absence, work out your own salvation with fear and trembling; for it is God who works in you both to will and to do for His good pleasure" (Phil. 2:12-13). It stands to reason that, yes, Christ has granted me salvation once I have accepted Him as my lord and personal savior, through his love-act, and have been baptized in His name; but I also have to do more personally by replicating His love-act by way of serving others in need.

Parents, without we creating a God-spirited home environment and its atmospheres in a young child's life, there is no way the child will grow and perform a love-act at will, in a secondary environment, let alone do things to God's good pleasure as a child of the Most High. I am reminded by something I have been taught, even as a born again in Sunday bible classes—to always pose the question, in the face of daunting challenges, "What would Jesus do?" Any person who has difficulty in any one of the four command statements discussed in the love-act will always have a difficult time relating to his or her world, at home and outside the home. In other words, building lasting relationships with positive impact in our homes and society can only happen when we live with the knowledge that love is, an (heavenly) act; until performed on the social theatrical stage, its true meaning will never be realized in our lives—remaining a mirage in our communities.

SECTION 6
Conclusion

E very family head needs to appreciate God's desire to have a lasting relationship with us, humans. God wants to relate at both individual and collective levels of our families, in spite of the separation we suffered through Adam's disobedience. He wants us to be, once again, part of His heavenly family, even while we are on earth. Therefore, he sent His Son, Jesus Christ, by virgin birth to us. Christ came to His own, but his own did not receive Him. As I have presented earlier, Christ was ready to leave His comfort zone, despite the immense riches of His Father. He was ready to leave his Father's estate behind and step outside the box by answering the Father's call to save a dying world—a call that demanded giving His life in exchange for our redemption from sin. We are a world estranged from His Father's love by way of the Adamic sin.

As family heads and authority figures, we also need to know that Jesus Christ lives in a relationship with His Father and the Holy Spirit—an unbreakable relationship forged in the crucible of trust and love, which He wants to share with us, and for us to also emulate His love-act and share with our children, families, friends, and coworkers, even strangers. Like His Father, He portrays and shares His love with us in ways that defy all human understanding. Christ values love and knows that humanity deserves love and needs to be loved. He is aware that we are of value more than any of the Father's creations in the universe; that is why He contrasts the Father's deep love for humanity with that of birds: "Look at the birds of the air, for they neither sow nor reap nor gather into barns; yet your heavenly father feeds them. Are you not of more value than they?" (Matt. 6:26). God's love for us cannot be bought, because Christ demonstrated that love by giving up His life on the cross at Golgotha.

God's love informs His actions and inactions toward us. Therefore, love is the standard that must inform our social-relational behavior and guide our judgment of what is important in our families and in our neighborhoods. If we, the heads and guardians in our families, wish for a better community, a better society, a better world, and seek a better life for ourselves and our children, then we must endeavor to model behaviors and principles that are in line with Christ's value assigned to love, as demonstrated in His love-act—the ability to give His all for anyone, regardless of who and what they are, and regardless of kinship. By so doing, we will infuse into the emotional character of our offspring the Good Samaritan ideal of love, which Christ spoke about in Luke 10:30–37.

The Good Samaritan ideal of love is characterized by a high degree of intense openness to receive others, and reach out simply because they are human and created in the likeness of God, and need to be treated with love, dignity and respect. It is an ideal, rich, vibrant, and sincere in every action or inaction taken by a human for the sake of a fellow human, regardless of race, ethnicity, economic or social background, religion or creed. It's an ideal that recognizes that the blood that flows from all our bodies is red and that each and every skin coloring is not determined by us but by God's own "rationally assigned cultural encoding, RACE" (Amagnoh 2014), designed to keep us safe in each of our environments, where we find ourselves on earth and nothing else.

To achieve the Good Samaritan ideal demands that we endeavor to constantly self-examine ourselves to make sure we do not stray from the spiritual and moral codes that God intended to govern our lives—to love God with all our hearts, minds and souls and to love our neighbor as ourselves. Adherence to the code demands constant prayer for God's grace and direction in the area of doing good to others, especially members of the faith. Our families need to be healthy in the values we uphold in order to inform, influence, and transform the kingdom community here on earth. As families of the Christian faith, we must develop and keep healthy values in the delivery of our love-act in order to impact the world and show the world the true nature of God through our deeds.

Christ revealed to us in the book of Matthew: "Brood of vipers! How can you, being evil, speak good things? For out of the abundance of the heart the mouth speaks" (Matt. 12:34). What this scripture tells us is that our words matter, and our words reveal the true nature and essence of our hearts. Our words reveal our inner motivations in life. And when we claim to be believers and followers of Christ, our words must reveal where our motivations come from, whether our words are based on the godly wisdom and knowledge of the fruits of the Spirit or on the wisdom that comes from worldly environmental activities. It is that simple; unkind words reveal a dark and unkind heart, while kind words inspire and reveal light—an open and kind heart.

A heart of kindness, or unkindness and hatred, is not acquired through hereditary; it is acquired by prolonged exposure to an environment that breeds and nurtures either kindness or hate. As parents, and social group leaders, we have a choice as to the home or social environment we want for ourselves and for our children to live and grow up in. Should it be an environment that shows love, speaks love, and acts with love, or should it be an environment full of hate, backbiting, gossip, anger, and rancor? Our final choice will determine the heart that exists within the authorizing environment of our families. That heart will mold and shape the personality and character of each child in the family; it is that heart that others will experience when they encounter anyone from our family environment.

The secondary environment in which we find ourselves as a leader, child, or worker does not matter; God is willing to take control of that environment, if only there is a heart ready to yield completely for Him to take-over. It means that fathers and mothers are to humble themselves first, (re)awaken the godly-relationship wherever it is absent, and forge a personal fellowship of communing with Christ in love, spirit, and in truth. We may then use that experience to relate with the children we are educating and training. In so doing, we will model behaviors, actions and inactions, edifying and commensurate to the Spirit of God. Then, and only then, will hearts be transformed through the wisdom and knowledge provided by the fruits of the Holy Spirit. Then and only then will we truly build relationships, creating and practicing social-relational value ends, as God intended for us and our families. Then and only then will we and our children reach out to others in the true Spirit of God the Father. Be safe, and stay blessed.

Congratulations! You have finished reading and studying about building relationships in the home, family, and society from the Godly and pointillist perspective. Please take some time to review the questions in practical activity 2. The questions may give you some insight into how far the book has influenced your thoughts, or if there has been any change in the way you would see others and deal with them moving forward.

PRACTICAL ACTIVITY 2

Organize yourselves into groups of two. After pairing, take a plain sheet of paper and a pencil and answer the following questions:

1. Has the information you received from reading this book changed the way you perceive or think and feel about yourself and others?
2. If yes, write down five ways in which the information has changed your perception about yourself and others (family, friends, colleagues, etc.).
3. If no, write down why the information has not changed your perception about yourself and others (family, friends, colleagues etc.)
4. Exchange your paper with your partner, and discuss the answers given with reference to the information in the book.

Note: If you read the book on your own, try to examine yourself by doing the following:

- Evaluate yourself, using items 1–3, above.

- Think about the ways in which the book has spoken to you in terms of how you used to perceive yourself and now.
- After reading this book, what are your feelings and thoughts about how to perceive and receive others, as well as organizing your home and family?
- How has this book influenced the social relational values you hold deep? Have those values changed in the way you see yourself building relationships going forward? If yes, in what ways or direction have the values changed? If no, why is that so? THANK YOU!

REFERENCES

Amagnoh, George. *What Do U See When U See Us? A Pointillist Perspective*. Republic of Moldova: LAP Lambert Academic Publishing, 2014.

Barack Obama Quotes. Goodreads.com. Goodreads Inc, 2021. https://www.goodreads.com/quotes/9609019, accessed January 29, 2021.

Eldridge, Michael. *Transforming Experience: John Dewey's Cultural Instrumentalism*. Nashville, TN: Vanderbilt University Press, 1998.

Gibson, Mel. *The Passion of the Christ*. United States: Icon Productions, 2004.

Herbert, Robert L. *Georges Seurat 1859–1891*. New York, NY: Metropolitan Museum of Art, 1991.

Hofstadter, Albert, and Richard Kuhns, eds. *Philosophies of Art and Beauty: Selected Readings in Aesthetics from Plato to Heidegger*. Chicago, IL: University of Chicago Press, 1976.

Hurlock, Elizabeth B. *Child Development*. New York: McGraw Hill Book, 1945.

Maya Angelou Quotes. BrainyQuote.com. BrainyMedia Inc, 2020. https://www.brainyquote.com/quotes/maya_angelou_578832, accessed November 20, 2020.

McCourt, Frank. *Angela's Ashes: A Memoir*. St. Louis, MO: Turtleback Books, 1999.

Moore, Mark H. *Creating Public Value: Strategic Management in Government*. London, England: Harvard University Press, 1997.

Nelsonword Bible: New King James Bible. Nashville, TN: Thomas Nelson, 1982.

Partanen, Eino, Teija Kujala, Mari Tervaniemi, and Minna Huotilainen. "Prenatal Music Exposure Induces Long-Term Neural Effects." PLoS ONE 8, no. 10 (2013). https://doi.org/10.1371/journal. pone.0078946.

Printed in the United States
by Baker & Taylor Publisher Services